How to Start a Successful Home-Based Freelance Bookkeeping and Tax Preparation Business

ℭℬ

Author: C. Pinheiro, EA, ABA®
Author: Gabrielle Fontaine, PB

Editor: Cynthia Sherwood, MSJ

PassKey Publications
Elk Grove, CA

Advance Praise for
How to Start a Successful Home-Based Freelance Bookkeeping and Tax Preparation Business

Very Informative!

I found the book to be very informative. It is a common sense, no nonsense read. I am sure it will be very helpful to many just starting out. It makes it so much easier to have all the steps laid out for you and organized. The tax prep chapter is good and, as a tax preparer, I am so pleased they clearly stated you need to take a tax prep class with an established company prior to doing taxes.

-TB, Las Vegas, NV

Clear and Very Helpful!

I got a lot out of this book. The authors use a clear writing style and offer many helpful ideas along with external references to additional sources of information on various topics. I would recommend this book to anyone starting a tax prep or bookkeeping business.

-EC, Fairfax, VA

Start Your Own Business

Good solid text for someone wanting to start a bookkeeping or tax practice. Down-to-earth, practical advice.

-D. Malin, MI

Other Books by PassKey Publications

The Enrolled Agent Tax Consulting Practice Guide: Learn How to Develop,
Market, and Operate
a Profitable Tax and IRS Representation Practice

The Chef's Commandments:
Maximize Your Kitchen's Profitability: Building and Maintaining a Successful,
Profit-Driven Restaurant

PassKey EA Review Complete: Individuals, Businesses, and Representation
IRS Enrolled Agent Exam Study Guide

ISBN 978-0-9818971-4-1

Fifth Printing, April 2010.

PassKey Publications, PO Box 580465, Elk Grove, CA 95758

A special thanks to:

Sylvia Jaumann and Mike Sheldon.
Thank you for sharing your bookkeeping stories with us.

Table of Contents

How to Start a Successful Home-Based Freelance Bookkeeping and Tax Preparation Business

ℭℬ

Chapter 1: An Introduction to Freelance Bookkeeping

This book is a genuine resource, packed with proven methods and valuable interviews with real bookkeepers and accounting professionals. These ideas and techniques show you how to quickly build a flourishing full-time or part-time bookkeeping or tax practice, and keep it running profitably. The authors have no financial interest in and receive no compensation from manufacturers of products or websites mentioned in this book.

Some of the topics covered in this volume:
- How to get started and obtain all necessary business licenses
- How to manage your cash flow for maximum profitability and business success
- How to find clients and keep them
- How to attract the most profitable clients
- How to increase referrals
- How to set and collect your fees
- How to offer tax services to your existing clients
- How to obtain referrals from CPA offices and other financial professionals
- How to become a Certified Bookkeeper through the *American Institute of Professional Bookkeepers* (AIPB)
- How to comply with the IRS recordkeeping requirements
- How to avoid your liability for the dreaded IRS "Trust Recovery Penalty"

"Have you built your castles in the air? Good! That's where they should be built. Now, go to work and build foundations under them." -Henry David Thoreau

Is one of your "castles in the air" being your own boss, doing work that you enjoy in the convenience of your own home? Do you desire to be available for your children while still making a substantial contribution to your household income? By following the path of those who have succeeded before you, you will begin the task of building a foundation for your vision.

This book assumes that you are at least seriously considering starting a freelance business as a bookkeeper or tax preparer. You've got better than average skills and you have decided to strike out on your own, or you have already been doing so for some time now and would like to maximize your business opportunities. Even if your skills are a bit rusty, you can take a short bookkeeping or tax course and become a full-charge bookkeeper and tax preparer.

Owning a home-based business is an enjoyable and rewarding experience, and reading this book will ensure that you are on the right path to a successful freelance bookkeeping business!

The growing number of small businesses ensures the increasing need for bookkeeping and tax professionals. While businesses are getting technologically savvy, they are not getting better at managing their finances.

Bookkeeping and tax preparation is something the majority of small businesses find intimidating. Even with the help of computer software, most people still hate preparing their tax returns and doing their own bookkeeping. Most business owners have neither the time nor the inclination to manage their own bookkeeping and tax reporting, and virtually every business owner needs some type of financial guidance. As a result, a freelance bookkeeping business is a great money-maker all year round. Bookkeepers and tax preparers do well even when the economy is poor, because business owners tend to watch their numbers more closely when cash flow is reduced.

If you enjoy bookkeeping, financial information, or taxes, you can become a freelance provider of these services. The fact that so many business owners dislike bookkeeping only contributes to the opportunities for anyone who enjoys bookkeeping and accounting.

Every business uses some type of bookkeeping, even if it's just a simple notebook with expenses and income. Bookkeeping services include bank reconciliations, monthly reports, daily entries, accounts payable, billing, and payroll. This is not to be confused with "accounting," which is not within the bookkeeper's scope. Accounting involves interpretation of formal financial statements for tax or reporting purposes. Most small businesses cannot afford to use an accounting firm for their monthly bookkeeping.

> Definition:
> *"Accountancy: is the statement of assurance about financial information. It is the art of recording, classifying, and summarizing in a significant manner and in terms of money, transactions, and events which are, in part at least, of a financial character, and interpreting the results thereof."*
> **-AICPA Committee on Terminology**

People often confuse formal accounting with bookkeeping and tax preparation. All of these bookkeeping and tax services are interrelated, but they are not the same. Bookkeepers and tax preparers keep records and report the client's information to the IRS. Accountants (CPAs), on the other hand, audit and analyze the client's information and report on its validity (assurance). There are some CPAs that specialize in taxation, as well.

A bookkeeping business can be started from home with a personal computer and a software program. These days, with e-mail and the Internet, bookkeeping services can be conducted almost entirely from home, although some clients prefer mobile bookkeepers at the client's location.

Working just twenty billable hours a week can generate a nice income. Many professional bookkeepers and tax preparers establish a few good clients and live exclusively off their part-time income. Some bookkeepers even provide tax services to their clients in addition to regular monthly bookkeeping, because tax preparation is so much easier when you have a client's books in order.

The key to learning how to start a successful freelance bookkeeping business is knowledge. If you have the skills to be a full-charge bookkeeper, you can start a freelance or home-based bookkeeping business. Even if you already work for a regular employer, you can market your skills to other businesses and generate part-time freelance income.

Truly profitable home businesses are skilled businesses—they require knowledge and background in order to be successful. If you have ambition and the basic understanding of bookkeeping and/or taxes, it's easy to generate income from a part-time bookkeeping business. What other skilled profession offers such great benefits so quickly?

Benefits of Service Businesses

Service businesses sell intangible products. Bookkeeping and tax services fall under this umbrella. Service businesses are more flexible than other businesses because they generally have a lower overhead, but you still need to identify what your costs are and your methods to set prices. Answer these questions honestly about your own potential bookkeeping and tax services business:

- Do you want to set your own hours and make your own business decisions?
- What are the key competitive factors in your industry?
- Have you decided what your hourly rates for bookkeeping or tax preparation will be?
- What methods will you use to set your hourly rate?
- How will you measure your productivity?
- Do you plan to subcontract out to other firms?
- What are your credit, payment, and collections policies and procedures?
- Do you have a strategy for keeping your client base?
- Do you genuinely enjoy bookkeeping and tax services?

If you have a good answer to most of these questions, a bookkeeping and tax services business may be right for you. Although we realize that what constitutes a "good income" is highly subjective, it is absolutely true that a freelance bookkeeper can make a higher hourly rate working independently rather than for an employer. This is true for full-time freelancers as well as part-time freelance bookkeepers. Even if you choose to keep your current job, you can still carve out nice additional income doing bookkeeping, tax preparation, or payroll part-time.

Freelance bookkeeping and tax businesses have a low startup cost. Most people already have a computer and a desk at home, and they only need to purchase software or an additional telephone line. Working just 20 billable hours a week can generate a nice income, and many professional bookkeepers and tax preparers establish a few good clients and live exclusively off their part-time income.

The Intuit© hourly rates survey reported that the average hourly rate charged for freelance bookkeeping was $62. Intuit reported that some companies even charge as much as $180 an hour! The average charge for a "flat rate" monthly bookkeeping service was $321 per month.

The U.S. Department of Labor Occupational Outlook Handbook states:

*"Demand for full-charge bookkeepers is expected to **increase**, because they can perform a wider variety of financial transactions, including payroll and billing. Certified Bookkeepers (CBs) and those with several years of accounting or bookkeeping experience who have demonstrated that they can handle a range of tasks will have the best job prospects."*

Most business owners have no way of evaluating a bookkeeper, so it is a good idea to consider bookkeeping certification. You can become a Certified Bookkeeper through the *American Institute of Professional Bookkeepers* (AIPB). There is no college degree requirement, but you must pass a four-part exam. Two parts of the CB exam are offered through Prometric (a national testing company). Prometric also administers the CPA exam and the IRS Enrolled Agent exam. There are a few other professional bookkeeping organizations, but the AIPB has been around the longest and tends to be the most recognized.

For certification, exam candidates must have at least two years of bookkeeping experience, pass the exam, and agree to adhere to a code of ethics. Bookkeepers that pass the AIPB certification program enjoy greater respect and higher pay.

If you were working for a temp agency, the agency would be billing your services at $30 per hour or higher. An employer who may not want to pay $15 to an employee will easily pay $30 an hour for a temp from an employment agency.

Why? Because they know that $30 per hour is the industry standard. As soon as you become a freelance accountant/bookkeeper, you remove yourself from the "employee" trap and you can start earning the money and respect that you deserve. Just look at the difference between the average hourly rates of an employee versus a freelance bookkeeper:

Average Bookkeeping Hourly Rates- Working for an employer	
California	$16.50
New York	$15.90
Washington	$14.50
Ohio	$13.12
Texas	$13.15
Wyoming	$11.76
Average Bookkeeping Hourly Rates- Working freelance	
California	$62.00
New York	$52.00
Washington	$35.00
Ohio	$30.00
Texas	$32.00
Wyoming	$29.00
Source: Various (classifieds) sources[1]	

Just Starting Out: Seven Basic Skills Required for Startup Businesses

Bookkeeping or Tax Preparation Skills

In order to start a freelancee bookkeeping business, you will need "above-average" bookkeeping skills. You must be able to do bookkeeping accurately and reliably. You don't need a college degree, but you do need to have some experience and specialized education. If you offer tax preparation services or payroll services, you need to remain up-to-date on changing tax law and reporting requirements. A few states now require tax preparers to have minimum education requirements and register with a state educational authority. We'll discuss this in more depth later in the book.

There are no state requirements for bookkeeping, but again, you'll find that becoming a Certified Bookkeeper through the AIPB impresses potential clients and allows you to charge a premium for services. People expect to spend more for someone who has a professional certification. Even if you do not have a college degree, there are multiple paths toward certification and they will be discussed later in this book.

Good Money Management Skills

While most home-based businesses are started without a lot of capital, you do need to understand how to manage the money that you do make. Track your spending and expenses carefully (with good bookkeeping!). Focus on your monthly income and be very conservative in the beginning with your purchases. Make sure that you bill your clients and collect payment in a timely manner. When clients are slow to pay, look for new clients to replace them. You're in business too—don't forget that your services are valuable and should be treated as such.

Self-Discipline

Since you will be self-employed, it's great that you won't have a boss breathing down your neck. But for some people, this is actually a bad thing! In order to be successful in a freelance business, you need to be able to have the motivation to work, promote yourself every day, and stick to a schedule.

Self-Marketing Skills

Self-promotion is essential to a successful financial business, especially at the beginning. Some people hate self-promotion, but we will cover a number of easy ways to promote your business online and in person. After your business is established, you will generate referrals and you may even have to turn away clients! We will discuss how to start generating bookkeeping clients and turn them into potential tax clients.

Strong Computer Skills

These days, it's impossible to do business as a bookkeeper without strong computer skills. Most of your small business clients are going to expect a computer-generated report and back-up files. The old green "ledger paper" is rarely used except in college classrooms. Take the time to become proficient in basic word processing and in using the Internet. You will also need to learn how to use bookkeeping software. The most popular bookkeeping software is **QuickBooks**. You may want to learn how to use **Quicken** and **Peachtree**, as well. These are two other popular bookkeeping programs that small businesses use.

Time Management Skills

You have to learn how to manage your time effectively in order to make your business grow, as well as have enough time to perform bookkeeping and tax services for your clients. Not all of your time will be billable time, especially at the beginning. You should count on spending about 15-20 percent of your time marketing your services and finding new leads. When your business reaches capacity, you will then need to choose whether or not you wish to grow. Will you continue to market your services? If so, you may need to hire an employee or take on subcontractors in order to help with the workload.

Everyone who owns a business has to manage interruptions. Some of these are beyond your control. Even in the most organized business setting, about 10 percent of the interruptions you experience are important enough that you may have to stop your work in order to attend to the problem. Practice techniques for reducing the remaining interruptions. Use voice-mail, and don't answer your cell phone every time a client calls. If the message is important, he or she will leave a message. Devise a standard for what qualifies as a reasonable interruption. Ask yourself—"is this really worth stopping my billable hours?" If you have a list of important clients, perhaps you can just answer inquiries from those few. The list should be short and the number of interruptions should be infrequent and important.

Watch Out for Burn-Out!

Early in my career, I (Christine) worked as an independent contractor for an accountant named Candace in San Diego. Candace was wildly successful—she had a thousand active clients and three satellite offices. She had a full-time support staff, but she still ran the day-to-day operations herself. She worked all the time.

When I interviewed with Candace for a contract position, I noticed a picture hanging on the wall. It was a photo of a beautiful Hawaiian beach. I asked Candace how many times she had vacationed there, and Candace replied, "Never! I simply don't have the time."

The following year, I opened my own practice and contacted Candace's receptionist, Nancy, to say I would not be returning. Nancy told me that Candace's practice had been sold after she had died of a massive heart attack. Candice never made it to that Hawaiian beach.

The moral of this story is: make time for yourself and your loved ones. Being successful means having the money and the time to live the life that you want. Success does not mean that you are so busy that you never have any free time for yourself.

There are many solutions to managing your time effectively. You are the ultimate arbiter of how much work or interruptions you will tolerate. If your schedule starts to get too hectic, step back, take a breath, and give yourself some time to recoup. You'll be glad you did.

Persistence and Drive

A vital element of running a successful business is persistence and drive. You have to believe that you can create a successful business from scratch, and follow through. If you have the strong desire to work for yourself and be your own boss, you can do it! Work hard, but don't suffer from "Weekend Syndrome." Most accountants and tax preparers work right through their weekends, especially during the busy season.

Make sure you leave time for yourself and your family; otherwise, burn-out will soon follow. Set aside some leisure time, especially during your busiest periods— it will keep your mind sharper and help you service your clients better. Mistakes will occur more frequently and your work quality will go down as you become more exhausted.

"Whether you think you can or whether you think you can't, you're right."
-Henry Ford

Chapter 2: Plan Your Business Strategy

It takes courage to start a business from scratch. The most important step is forming a well thought out business plan; do this at the very beginning, so you have a good idea how you are going to succeed. Businesses fail most often because of poor planning, not because the owner is unmotivated or lazy.

In formulating a clear business plan, ask yourself the following questions: How are you going to market your business? Who is your target audience? How will you support yourself while you get your business started?

All of this needs to be decided BEFORE you open your doors, not after. Your business plan should focus on how you will build your customer base and your practice. You have to determine what your startup costs are. This is where some serious budgeting comes into play.

What are the specific goals you want to accomplish? Why do you want to accomplish these goals? Knowing *why* you want what you do gives you the motivation and "juice" to stay focused on the results you are trying to create. Where will you be one year from now? How much money will you be making and how many hours will you be working?

Finally, now that you know where you want to go, what actions do you need to take right now to get you there? You may not know the exact answer, but remember, this is an adventure! So take your best guess and go from there. Because a strong business plan is so crucial in getting your business off to the right start, we've included a sample plan at the end of this book. You can also use a software program to write your business plan. **BusinessPlan Pro** is the most popular business-plan writing software.

The key to getting where you want to go is actually taking the first step. Give yourself a deadline for each action needed to reach your goals. Goals without deadlines and action are fantasies. Once you have written a basic plan for your business, it's time to start implementing it. It may be useful for you to keep your plan in a three-ring binder. As it evolves, you'll find yourself adding more pages with specific details and timetables for when you accomplish the actions leading to your goals. Your plan will become a living document. Breaking your longer-term goals into smaller chunks will make them easier to achieve. Consider what you will have to do on a quarterly basis to reach your goals. Then examine what you'll need to do on a monthly, weekly, and daily basis.

Once you start getting into the rhythm of setting and striving to reach your goals, you will build momentum and excitement. You may find that your business may not develop exactly as you planned it at the time you expect, but you will achieve results because your plan keeps you focused in the right direction. You will actually be building your own custom-made business and learning lots along the way.

Are you short on the money you need to start your business? If so, what are your financing options? Home-based businesses have a cheaper startup cost than traditional businesses, so you may be able to purchase all the things that you need with a small loan or on your credit card.

Deciding to Hang out Your Shingle

Starting out as a home-based bookkeeping business offers great benefits. You can operate your new business from a spare bedroom, a garage, or even from a corner of your living room! You don't need to rent an office or a store-front. You can do most of your work from home, even in your bedroom slippers, if you choose.

A home-based bookkeeping business can be started with a minimum investment. On the Internet, there are ways to advertise your services for free and dozens of ways to promote your business. You will be offering a service that every business needs, namely bookkeeping and tax services.

Many successful freelancers start out working part-time. Starting a part-time business (without quitting your job) has the advantage of still maintaining the benefits and security provided by your employer. Other freelance bookkeepers are homemakers looking for extra income. There are always pros and cons to starting a business. Here is a sample list of the benefits and disadvantages of working at home.

The Home Office

Advantages	Disadvantage
Easy setup	You must be self-disciplined
No commuting costs	Clients may perceive you as less professional
Flexible hours	Depending on your office setup, it may be difficult to meet with clients at your home
Available for family	Distractions or interruptions from family
Low overhead	Privacy and security of client information
Option to work on-site at a client's office	Social isolation

If you can overcome the disadvantages of working at a home office, you can anticipate great rewards. In a home-based bookkeeping business you can probably set up your office and business in a weekend. The money you save on renting a business office can go into purchasing a nice printer, computer, or other supplies.

You probably have many of these supplies already in your home. If this is the case, the majority of your investment is going to be your time.

If you have the space, it is best to set up your home office in a spare bedroom or other private space. Although people have started successful businesses from their living rooms, it is best to devote a specific area entirely to your business. There can be tax benefits to doing this as well. Having a private office will prevent distractions, increase your productivity, and improve confidentiality.

The fact that you are working from home without the added costs of a storefront means that you may well be able to start your bookkeeping business with less than a thousand dollars, especially if you already have a suitable computer.

To be competitive, you must invest in bookkeeping software, preferably the same software your clients are already using. Usually, this will be QuickBooks. There are many ways to get specialized training, and we will go over these resources later.

You will need computer equipment. You should consider getting professional stationary. Luckily, you can find new desktop computers and laptops far more inexpensively than in years past. These days, it's possible to find a new laptop computer on sale for around $500.

As for office furniture, you can purchase used furniture and desks by searching classified ads. Visit secondhand stores such as Goodwill and the Salvation Army; you might get lucky. You may also be able to purchase office furniture inexpensively at consignment stores. Sometimes thrift stores even have good deals on stationery and other office supplies.

The BIG 10: First Steps for Home-Based Success!

1. Choose a name for your business

If you want to do business under a fictitious business name, you will have to pay for a fictitious business name statement. This is also easily obtained from your local county or registrar's office. You do not need to file a fictitious business name statement if you use your own legal name as part of your business name.

Once you file the application for a fictitious business name, you will be required to publish the name in a local newspaper as well. If that sounds complicated, don't worry—there are literally dozens of newspapers that cater just to this type of classified ad and you will may get flyers in the mail from at a few of them. Your local county or registrar's office may also be able to recommend a local newspaper that will do the classified ad for you. The cost of filing a fictitious business name statement varies by the location, so check with your local municipality for the price and the required forms. You will have to renew your business name every five years, depending on the specific fees of your local government agency.

Example: Mary Smith wants to start her own bookkeeping service. She has three business names that she likes and needs to choose one. The first two choices do not require a fictitious business name statement because the names include her legal name. The third business name would require the filing of a fictitious business name statement.

Business Names Mary has Chosen:	
1. Smith's Speedy Bookkeeping Service	No statement required
2. Mary Smith's Marvelous Payroll Service	No statement required
3. A-Plus Bookkeeping Service	Fictitious business name statement required

2. Choose a Business Structure

When beginning a business, you must decide which form of business to use. The most common are sole proprietorships, partnerships, and corporations. The Internal Revenue Service has good definitions of each type of business entity in IRS **Publication 583**, *Starting a Business and Keeping Records*. You can download all IRS publications for free at the IRS website, ***www.irs.gov***.

You'll need to consider both legal and tax considerations when you're choosing a business structure. Only tax considerations are discussed in this book. You should consult with an attorney or an accountant if you have specific questions about business formation and your individual circumstances. Most bookkeepers start out as sole-proprietors.

3. Obtain a business license

It's easy to obtain a business license from your local office, and most applications can be completed by mail or online right at your taxing authority's website. There are online companies that will provide this service for you, but why spend the extra money? Usually it's as easy as going online and searching by your city or county name and "business license." If you have questions, you can usually call the city during normal business hours.

4. Open a separate checking account for your business

The best way to keep all your income and expenses in order is to open a separate bank account for your business income and expenses. Shop around—there are a lot of banks that offer free checking accounts. Choose a free account or an account with a low monthly fee.

Another way to track business expenses is to get a dedicated credit card just for your business purchases. Many credit cards offer good discounts, cash back, or airline miles. These are great perks for any business owner who occasionally has to travel.

You need to keep a proper set of accounting records for yourself, and keep the business finances separate from your personal finances. For example, if you are operating your business through your personal checking account and aren't keeping anything but the most minimal of records, the IRS may determine that many of your expenses are "personal" rather than business expenses.

Although you may be able to successfully defend your purchases in tax court—do you really want to go that far? Make your accounting task easier from the very beginning. Get a separate account for your bookkeeping business and make sure you keep good records.

Your business records should include copies of all invoices, as well as receipts for all of the merchandise and purchases you've made over the year. In addition you'll need to keep receipts for items such as shipping supplies and postage.

If you plan to travel to meet clients, keep a detailed log of your mileage. It's a tax deduction, and with high gas prices, you'll get a great tax break if you keep good records.

5. Set up your office and chart of accounts

Set up your own company right away with your accounting software. The most widely used bookkeeping software is QuickBooks. Most of your clients will use some version of QuickBooks, so you should anticipate purchasing this software every year. The cost for QuickBooks Pro is about $150-$200.[2] There are many ways to learn QuickBooks. You can take classes online, attend live classroom training, or use free tutorials to learn on your own.

To find out more about courses that teach how to use QuickBooks, go to ***www.Intuit.com***. The more you know about your accounting software, the easier your job will be and the more time you will have to generate income.

The second most widely used bookkeeping software is Peachtree Accounting. We've found Peachtree tends to be less user-friendly. It is used more often by CPAs and professional accountants, rather than the clients themselves. Although Peachtree is more difficult to use, it has a number of great features that set it apart from other software programs. A lot of construction firms use Peachtree because it handles job costing and billable time quite well. Peachtree also does a better job with inventory than QuickBooks does.

The price of both programs is about the same. At the beginning, it's probably best to concentrate on just one software program, but if you have the expertise to use both, then you will have an edge in the marketplace. You'll have a better chance of getting new clients if you have experience in multiple software platforms. If you want to specialize in the construction or building industry, you should learn Peachtree as well as QuickBooks.

6. Purchase professional business cards and letterhead

A nice business card and letterhead indicates professionalism and shows that you are serious about your business. When you send out correspondence, professional stationery is like a miniature advertisement.

If you have a good eye, you can use the templates provided by online stationery suppliers, such as ***www.VistaPrint.com,***[3] at very reasonable prices.[4]

Some consultants recommend that you purchase brochures right away. Brochure printing is more expensive, but there are multiple online companies that will allow you to customize and design your own brochure online. If you decide to print a brochure, make sure you know what type of services you plan to offer.

The brochure should include your name, address, phone number, fax number, website, and e-mail address. You should include a brief menu of services you provide. (There are samples at the back of this book.) Never include prices.

Professional business cards, letterhead, and brochures can make a good, professional impression on your prospects and clients, so take the time to do it right.

7. Get a separate phone number and fax line

A separate telephone number is highly suggested. It can be a cellular phone, land line, or VOIP line. Separate phone numbers may also be available as an add-on to your existing home landline with Distinctive Ring service from your phone company. You don't want customers calling you on your home phone number, especially on weekends or holidays. Some clients don't respect boundaries. It will save you from being abused by your clients who think that working at home means you're available to them for work 24/7. Having a separate business line also helps you appear more professional to your clients.

It is, however, important for your clients to have a reliable way to contact you in addition to e-mail. Do not let your children answer your business phone number! If your kids answer the phone and take messages, you may never get them, which will probably mean lost business. If you choose to keep specific business hours, you won't have to answer the phone at a time when you are "off duty." There will come a time when you will probably want to get another line, possibly for your fax and/or modem. But to start, make your existing resources do as much as possible for you to keep your expenses down.

Your fax machine is an important addition to your office because many clients still like to send faxed documents. You may choose to use a computer fax modem, which provides superior quality on the receiving fax. To send hard copies, you simply use your printer's scanner and then send them through the fax modem. But it's probably more convenient to have a dedicated fax machine to both transmit and receive faxed documents. That way, you don't have to remember to leave your computer on for extended periods, just in case a fax comes through.

Overall, a separate fax machine is flexible and convenient for the majority of faxing needs. Many fax machines are smart enough to work along with your answering machine so one phone line can do it all—voice, message, and fax. Most computer fax modems are not quite that intelligent! You decide what is best for you and let your needs and budget be your guide.

There are lots of good online fax companies that will allow you to set up an online fax number for less than 10 dollars a month. The concept is simple—the fax number routes the faxed paperwork directly to your e-mail, and you can print or save the documents. There's less wasted paper, and the cost is less than paying for a separate fax line from your regular phone company.

8. Join professional organizations

Because making business contacts though networking is so important to new businesses, it's important that you set aside at least $100 to join a few professional organizations. The Better Business Bureau, the Association of Professional Bookkeepers (AIPB), and the National Association of Tax Professionals (NATP) are all good organizations to join if you offer bookkeeping and tax services to clients.

You will receive information on events, continuing education, and networking opportunities. These memberships also add credibility to your business; the organization is essentially lending its credibility to you as a member. A few professional membership certificates can go a long way when you are trying to convince a client of your skills.

9. Set a reasonable work schedule

Even though you are essentially your own boss, it is important to set up a reasonable work schedule and stick to it. Your sanity and home life depend on your ability to keep your work and home life separate. This can be difficult for some home-based entrepreneurs—some find it hard to get motivated, and others don't know when to stop!

You should treat your new home-based business as a genuine business with set hours and a schedule. Although this will not always be easy, you should set firm boundaries for yourself as well as clients. If a client calls you late Sunday night for an Income Statement, realize that no CPA firm would be answering the phone or performing these duties for a client at this hour.

10. Prepare your home office

If you plan on seeing clients at your home, make sure your office is clean, organized, and free of clutter. Get a nice plant or good quality framed print. If your home office is full of books, clutter, or exercise equipment, seriously reconsider whether you should invite clients to your home. First impressions are important, and if potential clients see that you are unorganized, they are going to assume that your services are sloppy, too.

You home office should be isolated from family gathering places, away from the living room or kitchen. If you have the space, a small conference table is a good addition to a home office that accepts visitors. If you cannot give a professional impression when inviting clients to meet you in your home office, consider meeting them at their office or for a lunch meeting or at a local coffee shop instead.

When you set up your home office, make sure that you maximize privacy and minimize the possibility of distractions. If you feel that you will be distracted by family or noise, make sure that you can set aside private time to do your work. If you absolutely cannot get private time at home, you may have to invest in a commercial office—a huge expense for a startup. But you may be able to negotiate an office-share with another accountant, attorney, or similar professional.

Some businesses will rent small workspaces to bookkeepers. You will need to negotiate a fair amount for rent that is within your budget.

Make sure that your home office is secure. Since bookkeepers handle sensitive client information such as Social Security numbers and bank information, you must make sure that your client's information is doubly protected. For that reason, you should have a shredder in your office to properly dispose of any documents that include confidential information.

Be aware of your own safety as well. It may not be a good idea to accept strangers into your home when you are alone, especially if you are female. Consider investing in an alarm system. Some of the best security companies charge as little as $30 a month. It is an investment in your safety and security, and well worth the money.

You will want to tell your insurance agent that you are running a home-based business. An inexpensive rider can be added to your homeowners' policy so that in the event of a loss, your business equipment will be covered.

If you meet with clients at your home, you should also let your insurance agent know about that, because there may be some adjustments to the liability coverage you need, just in case a client slips and falls while visiting your home office. If your insurance company does not know you are running a business from your home, you may be denied coverage!

Startup Costs and Potential Revenue

You should dedicate at least ten hours a week to your bookkeeping business in order for it to be profitable, even if you're working another job full-time.

Startup Costs (Sample)

Items	Used or low end	New or High End
Desk and chair	$75	$550
Computer	$250	$1,500
Printer	$22	$350
Software suite (Word, Excel, etc.)	$250	$250
Accounting software	$190	$1,500
Business cards & stationery	$75	$450
Professional dues	$100	$250
Estimated startup costs	**$962**	**$4,850**

These are only theoretical example startup costs for a new bookkeeping and tax preparation business. If you already own a computer, desk, or chair, your costs will be lower. If you decide to purchase a used or discount computer, you will save money on your startup costs. The software will probably be your biggest expense, but you may be able to purchase older copies of the software at a discounted price at online auction sites like eBay. And if you are a student (even part-time) you may be able to get discounts on software as well.

At the time of this writing, students can purchase QuickBooks Pro at a 50 percent discount online and at most campus bookstores. A great website to purchase student copies of software is **www.AcademicSuperstore.com.** The software is the same, but there is a hefty student discount if you can prove current enrollment in even a single college course.

Office Setup

"Bare bones" items are what you need to successfully do your first job. Let your finances be your guide. Just remember, there's nothing wrong with the pay-as-you-go method; you don't really need the latest and greatest in hardware.

Buy what you need and the best you can afford, but no more. Remember, your business is supposed to support you, not the other way around. Think in terms of how long it will take for each new piece of equipment or software to more than pay for itself.

Here's a short list of what is probably "bare bones" in order to get started:
Computer with a fast modem, cable, DLS, or Wi-Fi connection

- Inkjet or laser printer
- Recent (legal) version of Microsoft Office; student editions are okay
- Accounting and/or tax software (QuickBooks Pro or higher is suggested)
- E-mail account that will allow you to attach files
- Separate telephone number with voice mail or an answering machine
- Fax machine or online equivalent
- Box of CDs and a couple of reams of copy paper
- Business cards and stationery

A few of the above items need some brief explanation. Your computer doesn't have to be cutting edge, but don't use a relic either. An Internet connection (NOT dial up if at all possible) is a must because e-mail has become invaluable in this field and long-distance work might be virtually impossible to find without one.

A printer is not as vital as it used to be since much of your work will be delivered via e-mail, CD, or flash drive. But some clients will still want their work in hardcopy as well.

A word about software: Buy a legal copy of all software, including Microsoft Office and QuickBooks. DO NOT borrow a friend's copy and use it in your business. Not only is this illegal, but it will be disastrous if something happens to your software while you are working on deadline with a huge project. Your client will be very upset if you are using a pirated copy, one that you do not have the legal license to be using. You won't be able to get tech support, and your friend may not be available! If you own the software, often a simple reinstall will solve the problems caused by an unexpected power outage or other problem that could mysteriously corrupt a file at the most crucial moment.

Consider using both a local back-up, and an online back-up service like Carbonite. Always make sure you have at least one digital copy of your back-up off-site, just in case of a disaster like a fire or a flood.

Chapter 3: Revenue and Hourly Rates

The revenue your business brings in will depend on the amount of billable hours and the hourly rate you set for services. For an average small business client, you can expect to spend about five to ten hours a month doing their books. This will vary based on the client's size, number of transactions, and your skills as a bookkeeper. As your skills improve, so will your speed, and you will be able to take on more clients.

Part-time bookkeepers might reasonably gross around $22,000 to $30,000 per year, while full-time bookkeepers may pull in $35,000 to $60,000 per year, and even more if they decide to hire employees. If you decide to offer tax services, payroll services, or other financial services, you can increase your billable rate even more.

The location of your business will impact your billable rate, but the most important factor in deciding how much to bill your client will be YOU. If you set a higher value to your skills, the clients will pay. Some bookkeepers prefer to bill a flat monthly fee based on services. Either way, you should always require an engagement letter and bill your clients according to the services agreed upon in that document. If your client wants to add services, make sure your client understands that additional services mean additional cost. It is better to have a single good client at a higher billable rate than multiple clients at a lower billable rate. Don't ever forget that you are offering an important service, and charge accordingly.

Income from Tax Preparation

Income from tax preparation is extremely seasonal. The majority of tax professionals who do tax work only face "cash flow" issues for the remainder of the year. Revenue from tax preparation peaks during March and April. Many professional tax preparers bill at rates that range from $50 to $100 per hour. CPA and Enrolled Agents typically bill at even higher rates, up to $400 per hour in some cases.[5] Tax preparation services are at times billed by the form instead of by the hour. This makes it possible to provide an estimated quote to new tax clients.

The precise number of tax preparers is unknown, but the IRS estimates that there are between 900,000 and 1.2 million professional tax preparers in the United States.[6]

Tax preparation is a good way to generate large revenues and a steady client base. On the other hand, bookkeeping and other accounting services provide a means to stabilize your yearly income and generate year-round revenues. That is why many freelance bookkeepers also offer tax preparation and vice versa.

Explain Your Fees Carefully and Concisely

Don't "nickel and dime" your clients. Charging for copies, postage, and other small items just infuriates people. Instead, include these small charges in your overall monthly bill, rather than itemizing every $2 to $3 charge. Offer estimates for monthly bookkeeping and payroll, or consider a flat fee for certain services. Marketing research has shown that one of the major issues clients have with their financial professionals is the breakdown of their fees.

Fees and Billing

Both authors charge a flat fee rate for monthly bookkeeping, but there are many bookkeepers that charge by the hour. You can also vary your fees based on the complexity of the client's situation. The average monthly rate for bookkeeping services is $345 per month. This amount will vary by location. For tax preparation, Gabrielle prefers to charge by the form, while Christy prefers to charge by the hour. There are pros and cons to each method.

If you choose to charge "by the form" you will be stuck charging an equal amount for a particular form, no matter what the complexity. But clients really appreciate knowing how much they will be charged. You can give them a price sheet based on the forms, and this pleases clients. Charging an hourly rate gives you more flexibility, but it also makes clients more uncomfortable. Fee disputes are one of the major reasons why clients leave a financial professional and start looking elsewhere.

Clients don't necessarily want something cheaper, but they want to understand what they are paying for. Consider creating a standard spreadsheet or another invoice that clearly outlines or describes the services you provide.

You may want to decide how you will charge your clients based on other factors, but remember that the IRS is very strict about some types of client billing. IRS Circular 230 outlines what a paid tax preparer may and may not do. With regard to fees, a paid tax preparer CANNOT:

- Charge a contingent fee based upon the amount of tax owed or refund due on an original return
- Guarantee a tax refund or guarantee that the taxpayer will not be audited by any government tax agency
- Negotiate or "cash" a client's refund check.
- Claim to give taxpayers an "instant tax refund" that is actually an interest-bearing loan unless that fact is disclosed to the taxpayer in accordance with federal and state law

Refund Anticipation Loans (RALs) are NOT a tax refund. An RAL is a high-interest loan against an anticipated tax refund. Any advertisement for an RAL must state conspicuously that the lender will charge a fee or interest, and it must identify the lender. If you decide to offer Refund Anticipation Loans to your tax clients, be aware that there are strict disclosure requirements for these types of loans.

Quality Control and Managing Your Expectations

Are you an extreme perfectionist? If you insist on perfection, you will burn out in a few short years. It might be time to question your quality standards. Are they actually too high? Mine (Gabrielle's) were.

I consider myself a recovering perfectionist. In the early days, I was deeply distressed when any of my clients ever found a minor error in my work. I attached my mistakes to my self worth and was emotionally wounded each time I erred, no matter how insignificant the mistake. It was a painful and unreasonable way to do business. In hindsight, my clients always showed appreciation for my conscientious work and usually took any minor errors in stride. I, on the other hand, was devastated. Too much of my time was wasted checking and rechecking my work to make sure everything was perfect.

As my client base grew, I began working eighteen-hour days, but I wasn't making much money because I was spending too much time "perfecting" my work. In my own mind, I had to be perfect. Of course, that level of effort was exhausting and brought little real satisfaction. I was setting myself up for disaster. As I started to burn out, I noticed a difference between what I expected of myself and what my clients expected. It was a huge gap.

Despite my fatigue, I still tried to do all the work myself. Eventually, however, I realized that I simply couldn't continue to do it all and take on new clients, too. Naively, I believed that all my colleagues who truly took pride in their work produced the same quality output that I did.

It was clear that I had to change my business strategy on two fronts if I was going to survive: First, I had to raise my prices to reflect the value my clients were receiving. Second, I needed to stop second-guessing the quality of my work and abilities. Not an easy task, since my expectations were still quite unrealistic. Over time, however, I learned to find a happy medium between perfection and the quality necessary to please my clients. You, too, will have to discover what your quality tolerance is and how you can identify others who share your philosophy and work ethic, should you decide to grow your business and hire employees or subcontractors.

Perfectionism seems to be a common plague in this industry, but it can be overcome.

What quality level is acceptable to you and, more importantly, to your clients? These questions are similar to those a financial planner recommending investment options might ask. An investor must know his or her own risk tolerance. Prioritize these essential qualities and know your minimum requirements, since the hard truth is you will not be able to produce perfect books every time.

Don't let the quest for perfectionism ruin your career or lock you into a low income situation. There is a fine line between trying to do good work for your clients and obsession over every potential error. That's what adjusting entries are for—nothing in bookkeeping is set in stone. You can always fix mistakes later. Do your best, but don't allow your freelance work to rule your life. If you become a slave to your hourly rate, you'll be exhausted and your friends and family will suffer, too.

Do quality work for quality clients, and if you hire help, they should have the same work ethic as you do. ALWAYS play win-win or no deal. That's the way to conduct business with high integrity, and not kill yourself in the process.

How to Set Your Hourly Rates

Once you decide to go it on your own, one of the most difficult decisions is figuring out what to charge for your services. It is natural to want to see just how much dough you can make working for yourself. So how much can you charge doing work as a freelancer?

The answer is: There are no set rules about pricing.

This chapter is designed to assist you in figuring out how much you can charge for your services. There are a few basic guiding principles many freelance bookkeepers use to arrive at a fair and reasonable price that will make a nice profit—and that is the real reason you're in business in the first place, to make a profit. Right? Being profitable should not be underrated, even for those of you who claim you don't need to "make a lot of money" to feel successful. One of the biggest mistakes made by businesses owners just starting out is they charging too little for their services.

You may think that you will get more business by keeping your prices low. And you may well be swamped with low paying work if you insist on being the cheapest in town, especially if you do high quality work. But you won't be making much money and you'll be exhausted for your efforts. If that is what you want, there are plenty of volunteer organizations that are in desperate need of your help! If you don't care about making a profit, then volunteer work will be far more satisfying than running your own business.

Okay, so you get the point and you are serious about making money. How do you know what to charge to make it worthwhile to work for yourself? In a word, it all comes down to time. That is why it's a good idea to always have an hourly rate in mind, even if you work with companies that want to pay you on a flat rate basis. All you really have to sell is your time, that is, the time it takes to do a job. It is true that the level of skill needed to complete the work should be reflected in your price. That is a good reason to charge different rates for different types of services, but ultimately it all comes down to what you are able to accomplish in a given amount of time. Everything takes time, no matter how efficient or skilled you are.

There are three basic areas you should consider in setting your hourly rates:

- The average wage for employees doing the same type of work in your area
- The operating expenses you will have to pay to "break even"
- The rates other successful freelance bookkeepers and tax professionals are charging for comparable services

Let's review each of these factors individually.

Most new bookkeepers are afraid to charge a reasonable rate for their services. Remember you are saving your clients the hassle and expense of hiring an employee. Your client does not have to pay unemployment insurance, worker's comp, or taxes on your wages, because you are an independent contractor providing your services to many clients.

CPA firms charge a premium for their services, and so can you—if you present yourself professionally to your client and have the experience and credentials behind you. If, on the other hand, you have some experience and training but don't yet feel qualified to charge a premium rate, you may want to consider subcontracting work from other bookkeeping services or CPA firms before seeking your own small business clients. Either way, you have value to offer those who hire you.

When you set your pricing, charge according to the value you can provide. One of the most common pitfalls for new bookkeepers is undervaluing their services. Charge a fair amount for what you provide from the very beginning. The clients that haggle over price are often the most difficult to deal with, or are the worst when it comes to paying late. Value what you do, and your clients will, too.

While some CPA offices offer small business bookkeeping, they typically charge rates higher than the average small business can afford. CPAs might charge between $100 and $350 dollars per hour. Even if your client uses a CPA for his tax preparation, many small businesses use the services of a bookkeeper for their monthly recordkeeping.

The 75 Percent Rule

Freelancers reason that they should be able to make the same salary working at home as they made when working for an employer. However, there are serious flaws in this line of reasoning. Even though you will generally have more flexibility and control over the hours you choose to work, you will have many bosses to answer to–your clients. You may also find yourself working when you'd rather be doing something else in order to meet tight deadlines.

In deciding what rates to charge, first find out the average salary for an employee who performs the same type of work you'll do as a freelancer. If you plan to subcontract payroll services, for example, an easy way to find out a salary range is to look in the Help Wanted section of your local newspaper. You could also call temporary employment agencies and see if they'll tell you how much per hour bookkeeping temps receive. There are online resources that publish average salary ranges, including www.salary.com that lists wages based on job description and area of the country.

Once you know what an employee is paid, you must add to that number the costs you'll have to bear because you are not an employee. This is crucial! It is known as the "75 Percent Rule."

When you are an employee, there is required work that may not directly contribute to the job you were hired to accomplish. For instance, you might need twenty minutes daily to keep your filing up to date, another thirty minutes to organize, choose, and order supplies for the office, or fifteen minutes at the end of each day to clear your desk and plan your work for the next day. As an employee, you would still be paid for your time to accomplish these "housekeeping" type tasks. As a self-employed professional, you must build that time into your hourly rate.

The 75 Percent Rule claims that only 75 percent of your working time is billable. In reality, that is quite generous. Most small service businesses have an actual billable rate of closer to 50 percent.

But we're being optimistic here, so let's follow the 75 Percent Rule through and see where we end up. The theory here is that at least 25 percent of your time will be spent doing work that supports the running of your business, but will not generate any direct income. These things include going to the bank to make deposits, sending out marketing materials, and doing general administrative tasks. Therefore, only 75 percent of your time will be billable to your clients, so you must add 25 percent to your base hourly amount to compensate.

As previously mentioned, a self-employed freelance bookkeeper will also pay more taxes than an employee. Self-employment tax (which are Social Security and Medicare taxes all rolled into one) represent approximately 15 percent of your net business income (profit). This means that as a self-employed worker, you will pay about 7.5 percent more in taxes than an employee.

Understanding the FICA

Social Security & Medicare = 15% of net income

Employee pays	7.5%	
Employer pays	7.5%	15%
Self-employed pay	15%	
	15 %	15%

Like everyone else, you will also have to pay federal and (if applicable) state and local income taxes. In general, an additional 15 to 20 percent of your profit is reasonable to expect to pay in income taxes, although this number depends on your tax bracket and varies by where you live. Therefore, in approximate terms, it is not unusual for a self-employed person to pay about one-third of profits in taxes alone.

If you are married and your spouse's employer provides your health insurance coverage, you won't have to worry about adding that cost to your rate. But if you are on your own or your circumstances change, especially if you have children, you will want to add the cost of your health insurance premiums to your price.

Now it's time to crunch a few numbers and see where it takes us. Let's use our example of a bookkeeper who, after doing a little research, can expect to make about $14.50 an hour as an employee. (See average rates listed in the Benefits of Service Businesses section.) Add the cost of non-billable time, additional taxes you have to pay for being self-employed, along with your health insurance premiums:

Base hourly rate	$14.50
25% Administrative, non-billable time	$3.63
7.5% Self-employment taxes	$1.36
Health insurance premium	$1.73
Preliminary hourly rate	$21.22

Now you are a little closer to making the same amount of money as an employee doing the same work. There is, however, another BIG piece to this puzzle to consider in determining your rates and keeping your business profitable for years to come.

The Cost of Doing Business

Running your business out of your home is definitely cheaper than having a separate commercial location. As a freelancer it is not necessary for you to have an address on Main Street, USA. So that's one cost you won't have to add to your price. It is also nice to know that you do get a tax break for running your business out of your house. Represented by a percentage of your entire living space, the area you allocate for your office entitles you to the Home Office Deduction. Consider that a bonus since you would most likely heat, light, and make mortgage payments for that space even if you didn't own your own business.

All businesses cost something to run. Your bookkeeping and tax service is no different. Much of your everyday operating expense will entail the supplies you use–things like paper, envelopes, toner, software, adding machine paper, and reference materials. There are other expenses, too. If you have a separate telephone number so your kids don't answer calls from your clients, that will cost you a few dollars a month, as will a voice-mail service.

Postage and delivery costs can be factored in if you will be working long distance. Business miles traveled to pick up and drop off local work will also add up. When calculating your cost of doing business, don't forget to include marketing and advertising costs, as well as dues to professional organizations such as AIPB and NATP.

Get Business Insurance

Another expense that is easy to forget, but very important to include in your costs, is business insurance. As mentioned in a previous section, if you own your house, you probably already carry homeowners' insurance. Likewise, if you rent, you may carry a renters policy (highly recommended). However, neither of these policies will cover your equipment or furniture used for business purposes if they are stolen, burned, or damaged by water.

You'll also need adequate liability insurance to cover accidents in your home related to your business. It's likely that your current insurance policy only protects you from being sued by someone who visits your home for a non-business purpose. If someone has an accident while visiting you on business, expect a denial of coverage if you didn't tell your agent about your business activities.

Make sure that you call your insurance agent and tell him about your new business, the equipment you use, and how much it would cost to replace these items if they were destroyed. Usually it is relatively inexpensive to add riders or endorsements to your current homeowners' policy to cover normal business risks. Be sure to get coverage for replacement cost and not just the actual cash value (depreciated value) of your business furniture and equipment. Needless to say, you must add the cost of additional business insurance to your calculation of your hourly rate.

Errors and Omissions Insurance

"Errors and Omissions" insurance is a type of insurance that covers you if you make a bookkeeping mistake or mistake during the preparation of tax returns. It is also a good idea to consider bonding. Everyone makes mistakes. We're all human. You have to protect yourself from claims, follow practices that will limit your liability, and carry liability insurance. This won't eliminate the risk, but it will help mitigate serious issues. Most financial professionals and attorneys carry some type of liability insurance against errors. Typical insurance coverage is designed to cover claims that are a result of practitioner errors or negligence.

The most common claims are for mistakes that occur during the preparation of tax returns. On average, claims settle for $15,000 to $40,000. Few claims exceed $500,000, but it does happen. In most cases, policy coverage is between $100,000 and $2 million. All CPA firms and attorneys carry liability insurance as a matter of course. Practitioners who sell insurance products or mutual funds typically purchase a separate policy to cover those activities. Insurance, real estate transactions, and securities transactions typically require an additional policy. In order to qualify for Errors and Omissions insurance, the majority of your income must be from tax preparation, bookkeeping, or other accounting services.

Arriving at an Hourly Rate

At this point you're starting to get an idea of the types of operating costs, otherwise known as overhead, that you can expect to pay to run your new business. Since you may not know exact costs, you must make your best guess to arrive at an amount to add to your hourly price to cover these expenses. So let's add a reasonable cost-per-hour amount to our previous example:

Preliminary hourly rate	$21.22
Operating expense estimate	$5.00
Revised hourly rate	$26.22

This example demonstrates how to arrive at an hourly rate that will compare to the wage an employee in your neighborhood receives to perform the same kind of work you will do as a freelancer. This is a way to find your "break even" price. Of course, what is not reflected in the 75 Percent Rule is that working for yourself requires A LOT more responsibility and skills than just putting in time as an employee. But we've included this formula to illustrate that there is more to pricing than simply coming up with an hourly rate.

We DO NOT suggest that you use the hourly rate here as your starting rate. You should use this guide to be sure that you NEVER make less than the amount you arrive at using the 75 Percent Rule so that you can afford to stay in business for the long haul. Otherwise, you would be better off as an employee!

Charge What the Market Will Bear

Once you calculate your "break even" rate, you need to remember that it is always subject to what a client is willing to pay you. This is especially so if you do not have much experience or training to justify more than basic bookkeeping data entry work.

If you decide to start off small with your freelance bookkeeping business and build your experience by subcontracting work from other bookkeepers or CPA firms, there can be a delicate negotiation dance when it comes to price. Subcontractors are not usually adept at negotiating. The firm you're contracting work from will want to pay you the lowest price possible to support its profit margin. But by using the 75 Percent Rule, you will know the minimum amount to start with in this kind of an arrangement.

When it comes to your asking price, here's an important habit to get into right from the start: Always ask for slightly more than what you think you can charge. That will give you some room to negotiate, if necessary.

Knowing what you are worth will help you be assertive about getting the best rate you can. True, in the beginning you may be willing to take anything you can get. We all make that mistake at first. Just don't build a reputation on being the cheapest bookkeeper around. Learn from your mistakes and know when to refuse work that won't meet your minimum rate. It is VERY likely to be much more trouble than it's worth.

Once you have established your hourly rates, you may want to adjust them over time. You'll learn if your prices are too low or too high and make adjustments when necessary. After you've worked with several clients, you will come to know who appreciates your work, is easy to work with, and is willing to pay you in a reasonable timeframe. Try to work with your best clients on a regular basis. Most important though, be sure you are making your "break even" price per hour–but usually much more– with the majority of your clients.

If you're uncomfortable asking for your rate, know that it gets easier with practice. You must believe in yourself and the value you have to offer. Otherwise, you'll probably be happier finding a job as an employee. Remember, you're in business to make money, on your terms.

The bottom line is to charge a rate that reflects the value you provide. You may be able to charge well above your "break even" rate, even in a tough economy. So charge as much as you feel comfortable with, and then add a little more. Your clients will let you know if they don't think it is a fair price. From there you can negotiate, if the client is worth it, and never dip below your "break even" number. It gets easier with practice.

How to Become an Freelancer

Why would you want to become an independent contractor, taking on work secondhand and having little contact with the company whose books you are working on? There are probably as many answers to this question as there are bookkeepers. Some may be similar to the reasons why you want to work for yourself in the first place:

- Flexible work schedule
- Being available for your kids
- Control over your earning potential
- Freedom to do the work you love
- Opportunity to learn new skills
- Variety
- Being your own boss

An added advantage of being an independent contractor or subcontractor (we use these terms interchangeably) is the fact that usually you won't have to deal with clients directly. That means you can literally work in your pajamas if you choose, without tarnishing your professional image! As an independent contractor, you're running a one-person business that performs work for other businesses.

Your clients may give you projects where you have a skill that they lack, such as budget consulting or expertise in QuickBooks software. You can build your business doing subcontracted work in a matter of months, or even weeks. The businesses you do bookkeeping for have to keep regular business hours. You can work when it is most convenient for you. They are on the front line, pulling in the sales, spending much of their time (non-billable hours) bringing in new business, while you are in the background, cranking out the work (billable hours).

Independent Contracting Defined

But what really is the difference between being an independent contractor and an employee? You will be working in your own office, probably from home, as opposed to the office of the bookkeeping service or CPA firm whose work you will be performing. You may offer on-site bookkeeping as well, but you should have multiple clients if you do so.

Does it really matter whether you call yourself an independent contractor or not, if you just want a bookkeeping job you can work from home?

The answer is a resounding YES! This is an often misunderstood distinction in our field. There is a very important difference between employees who work at home and those who are defined as independent contractors. The most financially important reason why you need to be clear on the differences has to do with taxes.

As noted in a previous section, an independent contractor is required to set aside and pay Social Security and Medicare taxes (otherwise known as self-employment tax) along with federal, state, and local (if applicable) income taxes. Estimated taxes often need to be paid on a quarterly basis.

This means you will have more control over your money than do employees whose taxes are immediately withheld from their paychecks. For employees, companies match and pay the portion of the Social Security and Medicare taxes that are withheld. Companies have to pay that half out of their own pockets. As an independent contractor, the whole amount comes out of your pocket. Bottom line–you pay all your own taxes.

So when taking on contract work from other bookkeepers or CPA firms, you must always remember that YOU ARE IN BUSINESS! If you just want to work at home and make money "under the table," you need to realize that you're breaking the law. It doesn't matter whether you do it full-time or part-time. Working illegally is not the way to build a good reputation or establish a successful business.

The Word "Contract" is There for a Reason!

When you take on work as an independent contractor, it is always a good idea to have some kind of written agreement, whether formal or informal, between you and the client sending you the work. Often this will be initiated by the bookkeeping service or CPA firm, but it is surprising–and a little frightening–how many businesses regularly hire independent contractors but have nothing in writing. Our best advice: Don't do it!

A written contract serves as a protection to both you and the primary service business. It also tells your clients that you are a professional and a responsible subcontractor—someone they can rely upon. That means you will be at the top of their list when they need your services. At the end of this book you will find a sample subcontracting agreement that you can use and modify to fit your circumstances.

The extent to which you are available is up to you. That's why you are called a freelance bookkeeper! You set your own hours and schedule. So when a bookkeeping service or CPA firm hires you to handle their overflow work, they should not dictate which hours of the day you will perform the work. If you work as an independent contractor, you will likely be working off-site, and setting your own work hours.

You may commit to a certain number of hours or they may guarantee you a set number of hours of work each month as part of your contract, but you will determine when you actually do the work. Some people are night owls and perform their work during the late evening into the wee hours of the morning. Others prefer to work while their children are at school. The point is that the business that subcontracts the work to you cannot tell you when to work, but only when the completed work is due.

In a subcontractor relationship, should you expect to receive employee-type benefits, such as insurance, vacation, sick days, or holiday pay?

No! You wouldn't pay your mechanic for being out sick and not fixing your car, would you? As an independent contractor, you are paid for the work you perform–nothing more and nothing less.

The expectations in your relationship with the primary bookkeeper or CPA firm are important. How much work they are obliged to provide you should be clearly defined in your contract, as well as how the relationship can be severed by either party.

Since you are in business for yourself, you should not become so comfortable with any subcontracting relationship that you fail to invoice your clients, yet expect to get paid. As a professional, you should invoice your clients on a regular basis, according to your contract.

Contracts: Are They Really Necessary?

"A verbal contract is not worth the paper it's written on."
-John Ledger

Without a written record, it can be difficult to prove what you have agreed to. If your deal goes south, you may be endlessly chasing the truth. Make it easy on yourself and write up an agreement.

Whether you're just starting out and only plan to subcontract work from other bookkeeping and CPA firms or whether you plan to build a bookkeeping and tax empire, you need to use contracts right from the start, without exception, both with your clients and with any subcontracted help you eventually send work out to. You should also use contracts if or when you hire employees.

In this section we will deal only with contracts in subcontracting situations, as well as engagement letters, which serve as contracts between you and your bookkeeping or tax preparation clients. The purpose of having a contract BEFORE the working relationship begins is to avoid the risk of problems and misunderstandings in the course of doing business.

Some resist using contracts because they feel it implies a lack of trust or because they're worried it may scare away new business. If you ask for a contract with a personal friend who becomes your bookkeeping or tax client, it may feel awkward, or even cold, to make them sign a contract. However, it is actually even more important to have a written agreement with those you know on a personal level. Nothing can destroy a friendship faster than business dealings "gone bad"! The purpose of a contract is to protect the interests of everyone involved. It is the glue that makes a win-win relationship stick.

If you think a verbal agreement is enough to build a smooth working relationship with your clients or subcontractors, think again. The problem with verbal agreements is that the only record of the contract lies in the memory of each party. There is no mechanism to assure that you each understand, in precisely the same way, the details of who is expected to do what and when. Even if you both start off the relationship on the same page, specific, agreed-upon details can easily be forgotten or distorted over time.

The perceived "rules" by which you each operate can change based on unexpected circumstances that might arise, which opens the door to assumptions and eventually painful misunderstandings. Unwritten promises are not easily enforceable and are a dangerous way to do business.

As the freelance bookkeeping and tax business owner, you bear the responsibility for your own success. Your clients look to you to get their work done right. Use written contracts with all your clients and your subcontracting relationships, and keep them up to date. That is the best way to avoid having your own horror story to tell when you meet up with other professional service providers.

What Will the Engagement Letter Cover?

Your agreement should include the scope of the work that will be performed on an ongoing basis, or specifically define the scope of any project-type work you may do for a client.

There are no rules here, but do remember the purpose of your engagement letter (contract). If clear communication is intended to protect you and your client, the language should be as specific and clear as possible.

So what exactly should be included in your engagement letter, whether you prefer to use a simple one-page letter or a multi-page legalese-type document?

1. The scope of the project or ongoing work
This includes the details of the exact results the client wants you to produce. Include the program format you want (QuickBooks, Peachtree, etc.) You should specify whether the client will be provided hard copy documents as well as computer files and how they will be delivered.

2. Deadline
You should give a specific date and time when you expect to finish the work for the client. It is also highly recommended that you include a time cushion for yourself when setting a deadline with your clients. Allow yourself enough time to complete the work and to do any tweaking necessary to meet your client's expectations. You will also want to state any responsibilities the client may have that will affect the deadline.

Example: "Bank Reconciliations will be delivered on or before the 7th of each month."

3. Fees
This is the area where the results of your negotiations with each client will be documented in detail. Whether you agree on an hourly rate, monthly fee, or an estimated range for a project, it should be clearly defined here. Some bookkeepers and tax preparers apply a tardiness discount to the rate paid by a client if that client does not deliver timely reports. If you choose to implement such a clause, it should be included in this section, as well as anywhere else in the contract you feel is appropriate.

4. Terms of payment
One of the most common complaints from freelancers is regarding timely payment for work performed. The quickest way to destroy your relationship with a client is to get angry when he or she is slow to pay for your services. Make sure you set clear expectations regarding retainers and payment terms. Consequences for late payment can include late fees or the right to stop services once a balance owed is past due. If the client knows your expectations BEFORE work begins, it will be much easier to collect your fees or to end a working relationship when necessary.

5. Confidentiality
It makes good sense to include a confidentiality clause in your written agreements. This gives your client reassurance that you will not release his or her financial information to a third party. This is especially important if your clients are involved with sensitive financial or medical information, and/or insurance claims. Any breach of confidential information is usually quite innocent, but

nonetheless it can be extremely damaging to both you and your client. Take the necessary precautions to protect yourself.

As a note here, if you do employ subcontractors, you will need to disclose this fact to your clients, if confidentiality is an issue for them.

6. Modifications and revisions

It is wise to include a line or two stating that all modifications and/or revisions to your initial written agreement should be mutually agreed upon and documented in writing. This is for your protection.

As you work with your client over time, you may wish to update your general contract to deal with situations and circumstances that may arise but were not anticipated when you began the engagement. By making revisions and modifications in writing, it will remind your clients that they are under contract and will encourage them to review their responsibilities in the relationship from time to time. Of course, this works both ways.

You might also want to include a clause indicating that if part of the agreement is not upheld it does not invalidate the rest of the agreement. This helps protect you if you ever get into a disagreement about who should do what as set forth in the contract. If it comes down to a "your word against mine" confrontation, you both lose. This type of clause might provide you a measure of protection in a bad situation.

7. Signatures of both parties

For your contract to be valid, both parties should sign and date the agreement and each should retain a copy of it. This indicates that there is a true meeting of the minds and that you both agree to the terms of the contract. There should be a statement to that effect just before the signature block of the document.

Making Your Contract Work in the Real World

Many freelancers do run their businesses without any contracts whatsoever. While we certainly do not recommend this risky mode of operation, it is important to realize that whatever type of agreement you establish with your clients and subcontractors, it must work in practical terms.

Your day-to-day operations should not be hindered by worrying whether you are adhering to every little detail of your contract. Your contract should protect you and your subcontractor without distracting you in doing what you do best. A simple one page, "bare bones" recap of the most important points that must be handled on a project may be the best overall choice for your business. Then again, it may not. Because of your client base, you may require a highly specific, court-proof, legally binding document to fully protect everyone involved. Ultimately, you decide what is best for you. No matter what type of contract you use, you must be able to live by it.

Be sure to fully discuss the terms of your contract with your client before it is signed. Remember, a good contract is about clear communication. If any misunderstandings do arise (no contract is perfect), learn from them and be willing to make the necessary adjustments in both your procedures and in the wording of your written agreements, if required. Invite open communication at the beginning, and you will likely avoid nasty surprises in the end.

Chapter 4: Sales and Marketing: How to Get Those New Clients!

The best source of clients is *referrals*. Once your business is established, most of your business will come from word-of-mouth. If you do a good job and offer a consistent level of professional service, clients will eventually come to you. However, when you first start out, you may have a difficult time believing you can find any clients as you operate out of your home office. Don't be discouraged! There are lots of great ways to drive clients to your business that don't cost a fortune.

Regular print advertising is usually too expensive for new businesses. But marketing yourself on the Internet is often free or inexpensive. In fact, the most successful marketing methods are often the least expensive.

Internet Classifieds for Marketing

You can expect to find one to two new clients a month just by using the classified ads in your local newspaper. You can also search job posting websites like Craigslist (*www.craigslist.com*) and CareerBuilder (*www.careerbuilder.com*). The best part of these websites is that they are FREE, and there are many to be found online.

The key is to search for businesses advertising for part-time bookkeeping help. Even if they're looking to hire an employee, send them an introduction letter and a list of your services. You may also want to prepare a sheet that shows how your fees could be more economical than the cost of hiring a part-time employee because the company would not have to pay benefits, employer's portion of Social Security and Medicare, unemployment taxes, or workers' compensation insurance.

A sample letter of introduction and list of services is included with this chapter. We do not recommend sending a price list. It's best to discuss your fees with your potential client when you know the scope of the work involved.

If you send out an introduction letter to twenty to thirty businesses per month, our experience suggests that you will receive an average of three inquiries and at least one new client. If you send your letter of introduction via e-mail, it doesn't cost you anything except a few minutes of your time.

For maximum results, you should follow up your correspondence with a telephone call, if contact information is provided in the ad.

Business Connections and Networking

Business connections are especially beneficial. Make sure you have quality stationery, business cards, and brochures when you attend events. Be visible in community business-related affairs (charity balls, cookouts, fundraisers). Join the local Chamber of Commerce and attend as many functions as you can.

Pass around your business cards and talk to people. Dress professionally (no sneakers, no jeans, no mini-skirts, no torn clothing). Business owners are always looking for financial advice.

This is a good time to say a word about targeting your clients. If you have experience in a particular industry, or know that you would like to work for certain types of businesses, you should focus your marketing efforts on attracting those types of clients.

If you have any connections to those industries through past business dealings or friends and acquaintances, now is the time to let them know that you have opened your own bookkeeping service. Networking is an incredibly powerful way to find new clients "out of the blue."

Realize that no two small businesses are alike. When you market your business, you should attempt to discover what a particular business owner really wants. Some business owners are most interested in keeping their inventory numbers perfect, while others want to do the bare minimum in order to file their tax returns.

Work with your clients and focus on their individual values, showing how you will contribute to their efforts to move their business forward.

Encourage your clients' entrepreneurial spirit. Tell them that you want to offer the support they need to reach their financial goals. After all, if a client's business fails, you lose a client.

You are your clients' partner in their journey to financial success, and you will become a trusted sounding board and even advisor in the process. This is an added benefit that your clients will greatly appreciate.

Referrals from CPA firms and Financial Planners

Some of the best sources of referrals are CPA firms and other financial professionals. Many CPA firms offer no bookkeeping services and choose instead to contract out these services to another provider.

You may want to send out an introductory letter or e-mail to some local CPA firms and financial planners in your area. The CPA will probably want to meet with you or at least verify that you have the qualifications to do the job.

It may seem like a lot of work to generate referrals this way, but if you can get even one CPA firm to refer bookkeeping services to you, it can lead to dozens of additional referrals over time.

As the CPA firm gains new clients, so will you. You may even be able to create a contractual agreement with the CPA firm to provide bookkeeping services to clients on a piecemeal basis. The busiest time for small accounting firms is usually during tax season (January through April), and a lot of firms hire part-time help to do bookkeeping and other tasks.

If you already have an established relationship, the CPA will come to you first to do bookkeeping for a client whose books are disorganized.

Start a Client E-Newsletter

An e-mail newsletter is one of the most effective yet inexpensive marketing tools available. As long as you have a valid e-mail address for a client, you can send them a newsletter. If you already have an existing relationship, it is a great way to keep in touch with your existing clients. You can purchase an easy template online and make your newsletter look professional.

An e-mail newsletter is an excellent marketing tool and serves as an educational tool as well as a contact method. A newsletter sent electronically costs you nothing, and it gives you the opportunity to highlight your knowledge and skills to your clients and potential clients.

A monthly newsletter takes a few hours of work, but the rewards can be enormous. If done correctly, the newsletter can build your reputation and prestige, and the resulting word-of-mouth referrals will more than make-up for your time spent.

Of course, if you have existing list of clients, send the newsletter to them, and ask if they can forward it to any friends or family that might be interested in your services. You must have people subscribe to your newsletter, if you will distribute it via e-mail.

IMPORTANT: You should use an e-mail service to manage your e-mail marketing. There are laws against sending unsolicited e-mail of a marketing nature, and you DO NOT want to attempt to send your newsletters from your own e-mail account, such as through Outlook.

Not only will you have difficulties when you list grows to more than about twenty addresses, you will also run into problems with your e-mail provider. Unsolicited marketing e-mails are SPAM and against the law!

You will need to subscribe to a newsletter and e-mail management service such as Aweber (*www.aweber.com*) or Constant Contact (*www.constantcontact.com*). These services are inexpensive and will keep you out of hot water with the spam laws. Anyone who subscribes to your list will use what is called an opt-in system. This means that they have given you permission to send them e-mail about your services. That is legal.

These services will also help ensure that your newsletter has an attractive look. The content of your newsletter should be geared toward your target audience and include information that is helpful to the readers; otherwise they will unsubscribe from your newsletter.

For example, if you specialize in bookkeeping for beauty salons, make sure that your newsletter includes good bookkeeping and financial tips geared toward beauty salon owners. Make your newsletters educational and informative. When potential clients read your newsletter, they should feel informed. The newsletter should not be filled with solicitation. Potential clients dislike an overload of sales type messages, just as we all do.

Be Smart When Using Direct Mail Marketing

It can be difficult and expensive to do a successful targeted mail campaign. We've found that just sending out fliers or postcards to businesses as a one-shot deal doesn't really work. But you can market intelligently if you have a plan.

Targeting New Business Owners

One of the smartest marketing ideas I've seen (Christine, here) came to me in the mail with my receipt for a fictitious business name. Let me explain. I had applied for a fictitious business name statement from the county.

Part of the filing requirement is that the statement be published in a newspaper of general circulation in the county in which the business is located. I ordered the ad from a small newspaper, and when the newspaper sent me the receipt, the envelope contained several fliers, including one from a local bookkeeper.

The flier was printed on fine stationery and a business card was included. It was a very intelligent marketing campaign. The bookkeeper was targeting new businesses exclusively. He knew that anyone filing for a fictitious business name was probably going to need a bookkeeper.

Using a standardized letter will save you time because it will require only minimal personalization in order to be effective. However, besides personally addressing the letter to your prospect (using the mail-merge function of your word processing software), you may want to mention something specific about your initial conversation in the first paragraph of your letter. That way your prospects will know that you wrote the letter to them personally when sending your information.

Always sign the letter with an original signature. It shows a personal touch. Addressing the envelope by hand also increases the chance that the client will open the letter, rather than just dumping it in the trash as junk mail.

Regardless of whether or not you get a response soon after sending your letter, it is a good idea to maintain an ongoing mailing list of prospects you would like to work with. Whenever you add a new service to your offerings, you will want to notify them.

Over time, they will come to feel that they "know" you and will either contact you directly or send others your way who are in need of your services.

Name recognition has a lot to do with successful marketing. After making an initial contact with a prospect, consistent follow-up will make your business success a reality. Regular postcard mailings are also an easy and relatively inexpensive way to consistently follow up and keep your name in front of your prospects, if you choose to go this route.

Here's a sample of a successful direct mail letter (always include your business card!)

BB INC.

Best Bookkeeper Inc.
123 Main St., Sacramento, CA 12345

At Best Bookkeeper Inc, we can take care of all your bookkeeping and payroll needs. Can you afford *not* to have a professional bookkeeper? Keep in mind that it is more costly to make mistakes than have it done professionally the first time. We want to help you concentrate on running your business instead of trying to stay on top of your books.

Our services include:
- Income tax preparation
- Accounts payable
- Bank reconciliations
- Input vendor invoices to payable system
- Request and maintain vendor W-9 information
- Respond to vendor inquiries about payment status
- Retrieve copies of payments as necessary
- Prepare and file required 1099 forms
- Reconcile vendor statements to accounts payable ledger
- Accounts receivable
- Complete payroll

Here are the benefits of outsourcing your bookkeeping services:
- Reduced overhead
- Avoid capital expenses
- Improved efficiency
- Save on training costs
- Cash flow analysis
- Minimize problems and receive access to personalized advice and skills

Call us for a consultation today! You'll be glad you did!

1-800-123-4560

Telephone Techniques: Smart Telemarketing

Making what is known as cold calls, if you've got the gumption for it, can be another very effective way to find new clients. Again, targeting the specific types of clients you would like to serve works well. Cold calling also tends to work best when you're looking for subcontracting overflow work.

The idea of making cold calls makes many people nervous. Isn't there an easier way? Yes, there are other ways to meet prospective clients that we'll discuss later, but the truth is, cold calls are one of most neglected yet surprisingly effective ways to get quick results. It really is not as hard as you imagine. The worst part is thinking about making the calls. So let's get past that stage right now!

Much of your apprehension may have to do with your own reaction to receiving bothersome calls from telemarketers who seem to call at the exact moment you sit down to dinner. Everyone hates dealing with the pushy caller who's trying to sell you double-insulated replacement windows or five more magazine subscriptions. Not only does the idea of making those kinds of calls yourself make you feel like a hypocrite, but you don't know if you can handle the massive rejection you're sure to face. Right? Well, you can breathe a great big sigh of relief. You are *not* a telemarketer!

As mentioned above, the best results from cold calls come when you're looking for subcontracting work—doing overload work for other bookkeeping services or CPA firms. The purpose of your call is to simply "touch base" with colleagues who actually want to know you're there for them when they're overloaded.

Believe it or not, they will usually be glad you called! In fact, many established successful bookkeeping services and CPA firms are always looking for reliable and proactive subcontractors they can count on in a pinch. The problem from their standpoint is finding you. If you do not already have connections with these potential sources of work, then taking a proactive approach is your best bet.

Okay, you're ready to give it a try and make a few calls. What should you say to these new potential sources of subcontracting work when you get them on the phone? A simple and straightforward approach works best.

You're calling them to introduce yourself and let them know about the type of work you can offer on an as-needed basis when they're overloaded or suddenly shorthanded. But remember that you're not really trying to sell yourself on the spot. It's always possible to get work immediately if your prospect is in a real jam and if your timing happens to be perfect. So make sure you're able to take on work right away, just in case.

But let's assume your first few calls are not so charmed. Your goal is to set up an appointment to meet briefly. If your prospects don't seem open to that idea just yet, offer to send your brochure and business card through the mail for their files so that your information will be handy when the need arises. Of course, you'll include a warm and benefits-laden letter of introduction with the promised information. Before ending the initial call, be sure to verify the prospective contact's name and address. Your entire call will only take about thirty to sixty seconds. That's all there is to it!

A typical call using the local telephone directory might go something like this:

Sample Marketing Call to a Potential Source of Subcontracted Work

Prospect: Good morning, CPA Accounting Services.

You: Hello. This is Bob Jones; may I please speak to the office manager?

Prospect: Speaking.

You: Good morning! I'm calling briefly to introduce myself because I'm currently doing freelance bookkeeping for companies like yours. My expertise is in small business payroll and QuickBooks. Are there times when your current staff is overloaded and you could use a little extra help to meet payroll deadlines or need someone who really knows QuickBooks?

Prospect: Well, we don't need a bookkeeper right now, but our regular bookkeeper is going on vacation next month...

You: That's fine. If it would be all right with you, I'd like to come by your office at a convenient time this week to drop off a list of my services and contact information, so you'll have it if you ever need to contact me. Would that be okay?

Prospect: Yes, that would be fine. We're always looking for people we can count on in a pinch, but I'm very busy today. When you come by, just leave the information with our receptionist.

You: Okay, I'll come by about 1:00 p.m. tomorrow. Will that work out all right?

Prospect: That would be perfect. What was your name again?

You: Bob Jones. And who am I speaking to?

Prospect: This is Mary Smith.

You: Thank you very much for taking the time to talk with me today, Ms. Smith. Hopefully I'll be able to say a quick hello to you tomorrow at 1:00 when I drop off the information. Just to confirm your address, it's 123 Main Street in Sacramento—is that correct?

Prospect: Yes, we're on the second floor, Suite 201.

You: Okay, great! Thanks again.

Prospect: Thank you. (End of call.)

That was easy! Of course, you might not do payroll, as mentioned in our example above. So you should create your own script to fit your expertise. Highlight the kind of work you would prefer to do and any other special skills you have. In targeting businesses, notice what services they offer in Yellow Pages' ads or the headings under which they're listed. This will give you an idea of the type of work they do and may need help with.

You will probably want to have your written script in front of you when you make your first few calls. Try not to read it word-for-word to your prospective clients because you don't want to sound mechanical, but if your mind goes blank, a quick written reminder will help you get back on track. You can even practice a couple times before making your first few calls just to get warmed up. The key is to *be yourself*. After you've had a little practice, you won't need your script anymore. In fact, you may even find that you like making these calls since you'll often get a positive response.

If you reach a prospect who is actively looking for a bookkeeper, your conversation may naturally last a bit longer than the sample dialogue above. Just be honest and friendly and don't be afraid to ask a few qualifying questions to learn more about your prospect's business.

However, be very cautious about quoting your price over the phone before actually meeting your prospect. You'll want to know as much as possible about the type of work involved, the turnaround time expected, and the form of work they want done before you negotiate a price. And since you've never worked with this person or company before, you'll have a greater chance of getting a fair price and building a good rapport if you meet in person to discuss specific project details.

So far we assume that you don't have a contact name at the prospect company, but if you do, by all means ask for that person at the outset. If that individual is not the right one to talk to, you will probably be told who is and you can proceed from there. Again, remember that you're simply trying to let your prospect know that you're a professional available to do work when they need it most, making it possible for them to take on more business without hiring more employees.

Live and in Person!

So you've got a few appointments to drop off your brochure and business cards around town. You're excited and terrified, all at the same time. What should you do to prepare for these scheduled appointments?

Present yourself in a professional manner. Even though the projects you will be doing will be coming to you secondhand (if you're looking to build a subcontracting relationship), you should still remember that they're your clients. Act professionally and you'll be treated professionally and paid professionally. First impressions make a lasting difference.

If you expect to make a professional impression you must look and act the part, even if you're working out of your home so that you can be there for your kids.

I (Gabrielle) cannot tell you how many times prospective subcontractors have shown up at my office to "talk business," looking like they were on their way to the gym or with two or three little ones in tow! I realize that there are times when you'll have to bring your kids with you when you're picking up or dropping off work, but DO NOT bring them when you first meet your new or prospective clients. It does not make a professional impression. Neither does showing up in a sweatshirt and sneakers.

Needless to say, I never gave work to subcontractors who gave me the impression that my assignments were only a hobby. Dress for the occasion and show up on time–and that includes when you're meeting with prospective clients who themselves are running their business from home.

When you arrive, plan to be yourself. Remember that your goal is to make contact and lay the groundwork for a mutually beneficial working relationship. This should be only a brief meeting, unless of course you've learned from your telephone conversation that your contact has an immediate need for your help.

When you actually meet with your contacts, be sure to smile. Let your contacts know that you appreciate that she took the time to meet with you. If she has a few minutes to talk, you can ask about the most pressing needs at the moment or the type of service that may be needed in the future. Try to get a feel for whether there's a good fit with what you have to offer and what your prospect might need. Take notes when appropriate. It will help you keep focused on the conversation and will be a valuable reference later. Inquire about the type of software used to assure compatibility. Keep your meeting informal and no longer than ten minutes. That's all it takes to make an outstanding first impression!

Now it's time to congratulate yourself. You've just accomplished the hardest thing you'll ever have to do in your business–promote yourself to someone you've never met before and live to tell the story! Like anything, it gets easier with practice. In fact, you'll most likely only have to go through this process a few times before you'll have more work than you can handle, since you'll quickly build a reputation as a true professional–a secret that will be hard for your clients to keep to themselves.

If you join a professional organization or a local Chamber of Commerce, attend the chapter meetings. When you do attend, always bring your business cards with you. More often than not, while in casual conversation with colleagues, you will want to exchange cards. You don't want to come up shorthanded. When networking, your most important focus should be on getting to know the other person and looking for ways that you can either assist his or her business or complement it by building a strategic alliance.

When Distance Is Not a Factor

Up until now our discussion has centered on finding work in your local area. However, with the Internet, fax lines, and overnight delivery services now routine for small and large businesses alike, is it reasonable to look outside of your local area for freelance work?

Without a doubt, the answer is a resounding YES! Technology brings "virtual" clients closer. There are some freelance bookkeepers who would not be in business without remote access to their clients through the Internet, telephone, and overnight delivery service. You can find long distance clients through the Internet.

Most freelance bookkeepers have at least one or two clients who are outside of their local area that they connect with via the Internet. Some never meet with their clients at all. If this type of work appeals to you, clients can be found through such sites as www.guru.com.

Doing business long distance can be especially beneficial if you live in a depressed economic area with low local average rates. Working with clients virtually means that you're not locked into those low rates. Your rates can be whatever your clients are willing to pay!

> "Guerilla marketing tactics? Well, when I started my business I wanted to do bookkeeping but I didn't have any money to advertise so what did I do? Every time I was driving to my office I would pick a different route. If I saw a new business I would park and go inside the business and introduce myself. I would ask them about their sales tax return, their payroll, etc.
>
> The best time to get a new client is when they are just starting because chances are that they still don't have a bookkeeper."
>
> **-Alfonso Lara, Founder of The Tax College**

Strategies to Bring in More Business

You can generate referrals from your existing clients. Are your clients aware of the different services or products you provide? If they aren't, how will they know when they need your services or products that they haven't used yet?

How will they tell someone else about your services and send you referrals? Good communication means increased revenues. No exceptions. It's a very simple principle, yet it's rarely put into action consistently and effectively. Every time you communicate with your clients, you have an opportunity to strengthen your relationship with them, foster loyalty, and encourage them to think of you often. That translates into more business from your clients and more referrals too. There are several effective ways to keep in touch with your clients, and a combination method is usually the most effective:

- Send out personalized greeting cards on special occasions.
- Save a stamp! Include a single-sheet flier highlighting a specific service or product when mailing statements or other regular correspondence to your clients.
- Pass along helpful tips to your clients by e-mail, and while you're at it, mention any new developments in your business such as your new website or a new service you're offering.
- Create a handy postcard listing your contact information and all of your service offerings and encourage your clients to save it for easy reference.
- Schedule a consistent client contact program with your favorite clients, and make at least one call per day just to check in with them to see how they're doing and say hello.

No matter which methods you choose, be sure to tell your clients how much you enjoy working with them. Mention that you would love more clients just like them. (Do this only to your best clients, of course.) Let them know that you'd welcome any referrals they send your way.

You will differentiate yourself in your clients' minds, and they will appreciate the personal attention from you. Just friendly, regular contact will often bring in more business and referrals in short order.

Chapter 5: Internet Marketing

Getting clients to find you on the web is only one way to bring in new business using the Internet. There are also sites where people look for professionals to handle their projects, and service providers (that's you) bid for those jobs.

The lowest bidder does not always win, but often price does matter. So does your reputation. You will need to build a decent profile on some of these sites, especially if there is much competition in your field. But this is a fast way to pull in new, paying work.

Get Free Publicity for your Business!

It's not difficult to receive free publicity. Afterward, you'll likely get a short-term burst of new business inquiries and possibly some long-term traffic to your website. In turn, that will give you a steady trickle of new business inquiries. Here are a few of the best methods we recommend for getting free publicity:

- Be a guest speaker or do a free seminar for your Chamber of Commerce or other local small business or industry organizations. If you're the outgoing type, this will give you valuable visibility as an expert in your community. If you offer supplementary informational products to attendees, you can also get paid for your efforts, as well as build your list of prospects.
- Write up a news release for any new services you are offering or any other newsworthy happenings within your business that may be of interest to your target market. Doing charity work or donating your services to community efforts will also get your name into the public eye – if you let the media know about it. News releases may not cause a sudden cash surge in your business, but it will support long-term recognition of you and your business, fueling long-term business growth.
- Write articles for online or offline publication. Editors of local weekly newspapers, trade journals, and online newsletters are hungry for useful content. Write brief, 300 to 800 word articles on subjects involving your expertise. Then offer them as free content to editors on a regular basis. You will build your credibility and pull more traffic to your website immediately. In all of your articles, be sure to include a bio or resource box that mentions your services and gives a link to your website.

Promote Your Services Online

In the 21st century, having a website is a necessity. Your website serves as your online brochure. It works for you twenty-four hours a day and is always there when a potential client wants to find information about who you are and what your business has to offer.

If you don't already have a website for your business, you need one. This can be done very inexpensively and will open possibilities for doing business without geographical restraints.

Your website will work best for you if it is simple. Your home page should be like a simple company brochure. It should be attractive and NOT about you, but all about the BENEFITS that your clients receive by working with you.

Your contact information should be easy to find. Include links to more specific information about your services and credibility. That's it! Keep it simple. The purpose of your website is to get prospective clients to contact you, (directly or via e-mail, to discuss how you can be of service to them. If you do have an e-mail newsletter, this is a great place for your clients to be able to opt-in and get a taste of what you have to offer without spending a dime.

Creating a website is easy. If you use a predesigned template, you can do it yourself in just a few hours. Many hosting companies have easy website software that uses "drag-and-drop" editing. What could be simpler?

If you're in a hurry and don't yet have your own website (which requires your own domain name and a hosting service – inexpensive, but takes a bit of time to set up), all is not lost. There are many social networking sites where, once you join, you're provided a profile page. You can use that as your temporary website if necessary.

Here are a few social networking sites to consider:

www.womanowned.com: For women business owners

www.meetup.com: This is where you can find targeted local groups to meet with for regular networking events, as well as create a profile page for your business.

www.linkedin.com: A popular social networking site

www.FaceBook.com: A popular, free social networking site

Even if you decide to use one of these networking services as a temporary website, you should eventually set up a dedicated website just for your bookkeeping business. It is more professional to have your own web address and dedicated site.

Use a Blog as Your Website

Another easy and quick way to put up your own business website is to use a blog. We recommend WordPress because it has many free website programs. WordPress is the best kept secret for a fast, easy, and cheap online presence that can give you a great looking site in less than an hour.

For the price of a Web hosting account (at the time of this printing, less than $5 a month!), you can have a do-it-yourself website. And you don't need the technical abilities of a programmer to do it either. In fact, I (Gabrielle here) have created several WordPress blogs myself that looked pretty decent, considering the fact that I really didn't know what I was doing when I created them. My popular blog The Freelance Bookkeeper (***www.TheFreelanceBookkeeper.com***) site is set up as a traditional blog (online newsletter/interactive web log), but the WordPress software has improved so much that you can now use blogs very effectively as your complete business website. You can have what looks like a traditional home page as the first page of your blog, and no one will be the wiser. It's a VERY easy way to get your own website up quickly.

Some of the advantages of using a WordPress blog over a static website are:

- You can add and update existing pages without the need for special technical skills or software, and the navigation and organization of the information on your website is updated automatically for you.
- It's an all-in-one solution. You can do everything a traditional Web page does AND have your own online newsletter to help your prospective clients get to know, like, and trust you, as well as highlight the services you offer, all on the same site.
- They pull in more traffic. If you update your website regularly, the search engines will send you traffic faster than a regular website. They just LOVE WordPress blogs.
- They are easy to customize. If you want special features added to your site, you'll find many, many mini-programs that can enhance and add functionality to your site, most of which are free or inexpensive. These are known as plug-ins and widgets.

Here's everything you need to put up your own site with a WordPress blog in just an hour or two: a domain name and a hosting account. That's it!

You can buy them separately if you like. Or if you use the hosting company I use, you can get your first domain name registered free when you open a new account. I use and highly recommend Lunar Pages because they have great customer service, they're reliable, and they offer a lot of what I need for the price. I've used them for several years now and have been very pleased with the results.

But if you'd rather shop around, be sure the hosting company you choose uses a C-Panel interface with Fantastico (which is where the WordPress software is available for free, along with many other free programs). You can also get WordPress software free by downloading it from *www.WordPress.org*. However, unless you are somewhat of a techie, I suggest you use Fantastico because it is the simplest way to set up and install the blog on your hosting account. It takes only a few clicks. Fantastico will also notify you and help you install software upgrades when they become available.

You could also get a blog without the need for a hosting account by using WordPress.com, where they will host your blog for you for free. But I don't recommend that. It makes you look less professional and gives you less control over your website. They have also been known to deactivate blogs without warning. WordPress is extremely popular, and tons of free support is available so that you can be up and running with your blog very quickly.

You can also choose to use ***www.Blogger.com***, which I (Christine) use for my blogs. Blogger is a simple and quick way to get a blog up and running. You can use it for your own professional diary, to run a blog for your business, or to promote your services to clients. Blogger is now owned by Google and is ranked in the top ten in the world in terms of website popularity. Best of all, it's still free.

Website Promotion

Having a website won't do you any good if no one sees it. You want to drive traffic to your website, but not just any traffic. You want people who are looking for your services so that you can bring in new cash-paying clients fast. You can accomplish this quickly and with little or no cost by using the following techniques. No one method will bring you a stampede of traffic, but using these techniques on a consistent basis will pay off in the long run.

E-mail Signature - Create a signature file that lists your company name and contact information, as well as any benefit-driven catch phrase that will draw everyone who reads your e-mails to learn more about your business and what you have to offer. Be sure to include an active link to your website. Every time you send out an e-mail, your e-signature is attached. It's a very easy way to be sure that everyone you come in contact with via e-mail knows about your business. It's a wonderful soft-sell tactic that works.

Online Message Signature - Using the same principle as an e-mail signature, include with your name a link to your website in all posts you may make to online blogs or message forums. You never know who might be reading your comments and may need your services.

List Your Website in Free Online Directories – Local directories are the phone books of today. Most of the popular Internet search engines have them. As of the writing of this report, both Google and Yahoo offer free listings in their local directories. Make sure you list your business in online directories while they are still free. In time, they will likely start to charge a fee to add your business to their listings.

Submit Your Website to the Search Engines – This takes a little time, but is worth it in the long run. While you're searching for local directories on the Internet, you should submit your website to the search engines. Eventually your URL (website address) will be added to their listings anyway, but that can take many months before it happens. You'll speed up the process a bit if you submit your URL directly.

Exchange Testimonials – Do you work with a business that you like? Why not approach the owner and offer to give her a testimonial? Ask that your full name and company name be listed, along with a link to your website. That's a true win-win situation since your service provider gets the testimonial and you get a free link to your website. Every little link helps.

Choose a Professional E-mail Address

When choosing your e-mail address, choose a professional-sounding e-mail for your business based on your name or business name. Do NOT use a "funny" or "cute" e-mail address. This looks ridiculous to a potential client and may cause a client to disregard your services altogether. It goes without saying that if your e-mail address contains anything "sexual," either overtly or not, it is totally inappropriate to use for your business. Here are some amusing examples:

SexyGirl@mail.com
VampireLord@mail.com
GoodGuyGoneBad@us.com
JediMaster269998@aol.com

None of these e-mail addresses are appropriate for a job application, business, or anything else other than communication with family and friends.

Also, never use a spouse's e-mail account. People will notice if your e-mail address is "BobJones@yahoo.com," but it's actually "Shirley Jones" who is contacting them. Since e-mail accounts are free through Yahoo and numerous other providers, there's no excuse for having an unprofessional e-mail address. Try some different variations until you get an e-mail that sounds professional and is easy to remember.

Hyphenated e-mail addresses are more difficult for clients to remember, and never pick an e-mail with intentionally misspelled words. This can mean lost business.

Avoid these common mistakes:

Bookkeeper_Sally@mail.com:
(Don't use a hyphen or underscore; it's hard for clients to remember.)

GreatBks@mail.com:
(See how "books" is intentionally abbreviated? This may be misspelled by a potential client.)

Sacramento-Finance@mail.com
(Once again, avoid the hyphen, and if you want to encourage out-of-state and virtual clients, avoid a city specific or regional e-mail address.)

Good examples might be:

BestBookkeeper@mail.com
HappyBookkeeping@mail.com
AccurateBooks@mail.com
SuperiorBookkeeper@mail.com
123BestBooks@yahoo.com

All of the above examples are easy to spell and easy to remember. Take the time to get a professional e-mail right away.

Advertising with Google AdWords

Google AdWords is an advertising tool on Google's advertising network. It's a cheap and easy way to advertise your bookkeeping and tax preparation services online. The ads can be customized to run only in your region, your city, or all over the United States.

YOU are the one advertising your product, and you design your ad! If you have a niche service such as bookkeeping for nonprofits, you can use Google AdWords to highlight your strengths and direct traffic to your website or blog, where potential clients can learn more about the services you offer.

I (Christy) advertised with Google AdWords almost immediately after I got my business license. I set up a "Starter Account" with Google, and set my monthly advertising budget at a maximum of $50 per month (about $2 maximum per day). You can decide on a daily and monthly maximum. Once you top out your advertising budget, your ad stops running.

After establishing your starter account, you need to create your ads. You create sample ads and choose keywords, which are words or phrases related to your business. You can find keyword ideas on the web. Just look up your competitors' websites.

Google ads work when someone enters your keywords into Google's search engines. Your ads then appear next to the search results. Your ad may not show up all the time—ads are all rotated by Google. The benefit is that you're advertising to an audience who's already interested in you. You are charged only when someone clicks on your ad.

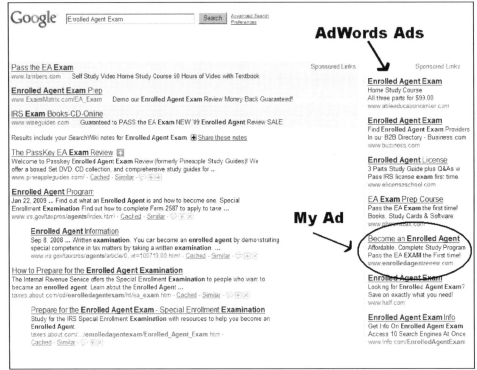

Christy's Ads on Google AdWords

How Google AdWords Works:
- You create ads and choose keywords, which are words or phrases related to your business. Get keyword ideas by looking on the web for other ads.
- Your ads appear on Google. When people search on Google using one of your keywords, your ad may appear next to the search results.
- You attract clients. People can simply click on your ad to learn more about you. If you don't have a website yet, Google will also help you create a website for free.
- People click on your ad to learn more about your services. You don't even need a webpage to join AdWords– Google will help you create one for free.

No matter what your budget, you can display ads on Google and their advertising network. You pay only if people click your ads. To sign up, go to ***www.adwords.google.com.***

I (Christy) personally believe that the majority of my referrals come from my click ads on Google. When people search for study guides for the IRS Enrolled Agent exam, my ad pops up and takes potential customers to my website. I pay a fee only when a user actually "clicks" on the ad. The reports on my website reflect that the majority of the traffic is generated from Google advertising.

I check my traffic reports frequently. This is something you should learn to do.

Take some time to research Google's AdWords program for yourself. You can also try out different ads to see which ones generate the most traffic and sales on your website. And you never have to spend more than what your budget allows.

Create a Free Online Google Profile

Google is the Internet juggernaut. You can control how you appear in Google by creating a personal profile. You can use any e-mail address to form a Google account. If you already belong to a Google Group, then you already have an existing profile. You just need to set it up!

In less than a few days, your public profile will be bumped to the top of Google's search engines. When anyone searches for your name on Google, your profile will pop up and all of your websites and your bio will be displayed. As I mentioned before, make sure you use your real name or business name so your clients can find you. It's free to create a Google profile, so create one right away. Make sure you list all your websites in your Google profile. If you have a blog, website, or even just a Facebook page, list the URL.

You probably have a Google account already if you belong to any Google Newsgroups or if you have already signed up for Google AdWords. If you want to create a completely different Google account using a new e-mail or password, you can do that too. You can post photos of yourself or photos of your business.

Chapter 6: How About Professional Bookkeeper Certification?

You may want to consider professional certification from the American Institute of Professional Bookkeepers. The AIPB is the bookkeeping profession's national association. The additional respect and potential income that professional certification provides is worth the effort. The Certified Bookkeeper Designation adds to your marketability and assures any potential client or employer that you have a certain level of skills necessary for the job.

You do not have to have a degree, but you must pass a four-part exam on bookkeeping. The requirements to become a certified bookkeeper through the AIPB are as follows:

AIPB Candidate Requirements

Experience: At least two years full-time experience or the part-time or freelance equivalent.

Examination: Candidates must pass a four-part national examination, including two parts given at any Prometric Test Center (there are over 300 nationwide).

Code of Ethics: Applicants must sign a Code of Ethics.

The certification exam consists of four parts:

Part 1—at Prometric
Testlet 1: Adjusting entries. One hour.
Testlet 2: Error correction (includes bank reconciliation.) One hour.

Part 2—at Prometric
Testlet 1: Payroll. One hour.
Testlet 2: Depreciation. One hour.

Part 3—Through the AIPB
Open workbook test
Inventory

Part 4—Through the AIPB
Open workbook test
Internal controls and fraud prevention

Preparing for the AIPB Certification Exam

The AIPB offers optional self-teaching workbooks that prepare you for each part of the exam. Each workbook drills you with questions like those on the certification exam. All questions at Prometric and in the workbook are multiple choice. The passing score for each part of each test at Prometric is 75 percent, and for each open book workbook test is 70 percent. An applicant who receives a lower grade can schedule a retest.

AIPB's mission is to achieve recognition of bookkeepers as accounting professionals; keep bookkeepers up to date on changes in bookkeeping, accounting and tax issues; answer bookkeepers' everyday bookkeeping and accounting questions; and certify bookkeepers who meet high, national standards. Once a candidate passes the exam and experience requirements, he or she earns the right to add "CB" (Certified Bookkeeper) to his or her name.

Founded in 1987, the AIPB's mission is to raise the professional status of bookkeepers. Its current membership is 30,000 bookkeeping professionals.

"Small businesses often have only a bookkeeper as their sole financial officer. Now they can rely on that de facto CFO as a highly qualified and certified expert, complete with the experience, training, and qualifications provided by a program established by the American Institute of Professional Bookkeepers (www.aipb.org)."

-Atlanta Journal and Constitution

"Certified Bookkeepers are one of the most critical positions within any organization, but most especially for the small business owner," says Financial Consultant Anita Johnson. "This isn't about data entry, this is about payroll, accruals, deferrals, adjusting trial balances, calculating depreciation, and valuation of merchandise inventory. It's the entire package. And if you're certified, you become tremendously valuable."

-The Sacramento Bee

"Certified Bookkeepers demonstrate not only a proven knowledge of basic GAAP accounting," says Margaret Stone, Pima Community College, (AZ), "but the motivation to learn and the desire and ambition to be a professional."
-Internal Auditing Report newsletter, Warren Gorham Lamont

AIPB's certification program is the first and only national standard for bookkeeping in America—a high standard in advanced bookkeeping.

Over 200 colleges offer AIPB's course in advanced bookkeeping to prepare bookkeepers for the national certification exam. There are also many bookkeepers who prepare for the exam on their own.

"Certified Bookkeepers are doing for accounting what paralegals did for law and physicians' assistants did for medicine— but at a higher level. More importantly, anyone who becomes a Certified Bookkeeper is eminently trainable for industry specialization, tax preparation, or more advanced accounting. By becoming certified, they have demonstrated not only a proven knowledge of basic GAAP accounting, but the motivation to learn and the desire and ambition to be a professional."

-Margaret A. Johnson, CB
Certified Bookkeeper and Instructor
Pima Community College, Tucson AZ.

Contact information for the AIPB:

American Institute of Professional Bookkeepers
Suite 500, 6001 Montrose Road
Rockville, MD 20852
Telephone: 800-622-0121
Fax: 800-541-0066,
E-mail: info@aipb.org.
Website: ***www.aipb.org***

How to Become a Certified QuickBooks ProAdvisor®

Costs: ProAdvisor Membership
One Year: $449
With optional Payroll: $599

A great way to increase your referrals and credibility in the marketplace is to become a Certified QuickBooks ProAdvisor®. This is a certification and exam offered and administered by Intuit, the manufacturer of QuickBooks software. To sign up, you will need to call (888) 236-9501. You have to talk to an Intuit employee in order to sign up for the program.

The courses are available online and are self-study. The primary certification course is designed for bookkeepers and accounting professionals who already have a good working knowledge of QuickBooks and bookkeeping. A degree is not required. To take the course, you should be comfortable working with QuickBooks' lists, forms, registers, and reports. You should be able to set up a company data file, manage accounts receivable and accounts payable, track sales tax, enter inventory, track time, work with payroll items, and reconcile accounts.

To become a Certified QuickBooks ProAdvisor®, you must complete the online testing after each section and receive a score of 85 percent or better.

Generally, certification takes about sixteen hours, but the time and investment is well worth the effort. Bookkeepers who have taken the ProAdvisor® courses and obtained certification are glad they did. That's because once certified, each ProAdvisor is given a free listing and customizable profile page in the QuickBooks searchable directory, which Intuit markets aggressively. That means referrals for business from qualified prospects, based on your geographic location.

There are several additional certification courses available in the ProAdvisor program, but the initial certification course is well balanced. Anyone familiar with the basics of QuickBooks who also has a good knowledge of bookkeeping should have little trouble passing the course. Less experienced bookkeepers would benefit from the extra knowledge if they're willing to dig into the software to really learn how to be proficient with it.

The additional certification courses available in the program cover Advanced Certification in QuickBooks, Certification in Enterprise Solutions, as well as the QuickBooks Point of Sale system.

The course is a good overview and a worthwhile investment for bookkeepers looking to obtain certifications and enhance their own practice. This certification makes a bookkeeper more marketable to clients and businesses, and certification generates referrals directly from Intuit.

Additionally, there are educational and marketing resources available to those in the ProAdvisor program, as well as copies of the QuickBooks Premier Accountant Edition and Enterprise Edition at no additional charge. ProAdvisors are also given a priority technical support telephone number and early notification of new programs and upgrades.

Chapter 7: Offering Other Financial Services

One of the best ways to increase revenue is to diversify your services. Become a full-service provider. Listen to your clients and add services based on their needs. Eighty-five percent of small businesses have fewer than twenty employees. These small businesses usually want the easiest solution to their bookkeeping and financial reporting requirements.

Most small businesses would love to have one place to go for payroll, tax preparation, sales tax reporting, bookkeeping, and financial statements. The best part about offering these additional services is that they generate revenue all year round. Tax preparation is a good way to generate large revenues and a steady client base. On the other hand, bookkeeping and other financial services provide a stable yearly income and generate year-round revenues.

Why not make your practice a "one-stop" shop? Always explain all the other valuable financial services you offer. Have a brochure ready and make sure every potential client knows that your office is their "one-stop" shop. You can even consider offering insurance services and real estate representation, if you obtain the necessary licenses to do so.

Offering Payroll Services

Accounting and tax professionals usually have strong feelings about payroll. Some offer payroll services but dislike doing payroll, and some professionals do payroll for dozens of clients and love how easy it is to offer the service.

> *"Payroll is a business by itself. I'm fine doing payroll because I discovered PayCycle (payroll software on the Internet) a few years ago and they really make payroll not only easy but affordable to the professional preparer."*
> **-Alfonso Lara, Founder of The Tax College**

One way to offer payroll services to multiple clients is to set up an account with an Internet payroll service provider. Most Internet payroll companies have special discounts just for accounting professionals. This makes it easy to offer an affordable payroll service to small and mid-sized businesses.

There are numerous companies that have accounting professional plans.

Offering Tax Services

Offering tax services is an easy way to expand a bookkeeping business. You have the client's financial information already, so it's a natural progression to offer tax services. Tax services are more lucrative, but the work is seasonal. Most tax professionals charge an average of $150 to $350 for an individual return and even higher for business returns. In most states, you don't need any special education to become a tax preparer. However, this is going to change.

Two states, California and Oregon, already require that tax preparers have minimum educational requirements, and the rest of the states are expected to follow suit. Some people believe that tax professionals must have a college degree or be CPAs. However, this is not the case. Requirements for certification and licensing can vary from state to state, so it is important to research and be aware of local requirements. We will discuss the requirements for California and Oregon later in this book.

Currently, the IRS is working on a plan to require registration for all tax professionals. This is expected to start sometime between 2011 and 2012. If you decide to offer tax services, it might be a good idea to start researching your educational options right away, so you can be prepared when the new rules go into effect.

Get Training & Experience

The least expensive way to become a tax preparer is to take an introductory course with established tax return preparation companies like Jackson Hewitt or H&R Block. These firms have an established course that can be completed in a few months. At the end of your training, you can work for them and gain valuable experience. The advantage to these courses is they are inexpensive and you will learn how to prepare tax returns by hand. That means you use paper, pencil, and a calculator.

The disadvantage to them is that you will not learn how to use any professional tax preparation software. If you choose to work for the company that administers the class, you will only be introduced to their "interview" software that each company uses for its own tax preparation services.

If you are interested in taking these classes, they usually begin in the fall and run through the end of November in preparation for the upcoming tax season. Another training option is to take a correspondence or online course. There are several independent companies that offer distance courses for individuals that wish to become tax preparers. It's a good idea to have some real experience before you start offering tax preparation. A good marker is a minimum of two seasons ("tax season" runs from January to April 15) of tax experience and general knowledge of tax preparation.

A great way to get this experience is working for an independent tax professional during tax season. Just a few weeks of experience can go a long way toward knowing what's really involved in offering this type of service to your clients. A small CPA firm or independent Enrolled Agent office can help you get the hands-on experience you need with a safety net to have someone else checking your work before you venture out on your own as a tax professional.

Once you've finished your training and gained some experience, you'll be ready to start offering tax preparation services as an additional profit center to your business. Tax preparation is generally seasonal, but is a nice boost to your bottom line because it is billed at a much higher rate.

Some established tax preparers work only four months a year, during tax season, and generate enough revenue so that they don't need to work the rest of the year. This usually means they have a large, established client base, but there is no reason you can't start building your client list from your existing bookkeeping client base.

Tax Preparation Software

There are numerous choices for tax preparation software. Gabrielle likes Intuit's ProSeries and Christine uses Lacerte.

You can invest in a more expensive suite like Lacerte, and use their single license. Then you pay for the software and a fee whenever you file a tax return. This is called a pay-per-use license. Lacerte and ProSeries are two of the best in the marketplace, but if they're too expensive, you can also try a less expensive software suite.

TaxAct is easy to use and is less than $200 for a professional version of their Individual (Form 1040) software. Their business suite for filing partnership and corporate tax returns is under $700. If you're on a tight budget or you do fewer than 100 tax returns per year, try TaxAct. See if you can get a "demo" version of the software to try. Tax software companies are often glad to give new practitioners a demo version of their software (usually last year's version) so you can try it out. When you get the demo versions, prepare a few "dummy returns" and see which software you like the best.

Electronic Filing

If you decide to offer tax services, you will need to apply to become an IRS e-file Provider. These days, most tax returns are filed electronically. To be able to transmit tax returns to the IRS electronically, you will need to apply to become an "ERO" (Electronic Return Originator).

Although it may seem complicated a first, it's really not as hard as it seems, and you only have to go though the hassle once. First, you should read **Publication 3112**, *IRS e-file Application and Participation*. You will have to register online at IRS e-services. Go to ***www.irs.gov*** and click on the "tax professionals" link in order to get more information on IRS e-services.

You must complete your IRS e-file application online, after registering or logging on to e-services. Authorized e-file Providers who are active participants in IRS e-file and who e-file five or more accepted individual or business tax returns in a calendar year can use IRS e-services. Once you complete the online application, you'll receive instructions on how to complete your registration.

You will have to pass a background check, which includes fingerprinting, and you will have to pass an IRS "suitability check," meaning that the IRS will check to see if you are in compliance with your own personal tax returns.

The IRS "suitability check" may include the following:
- An FBI criminal background check
- A credit history check
- An IRS records check to ensure that all individual and business returns are filed, and balance paid or appropriately addressed; and identify instances of fraud and preparer penalties
- A history check for prior noncompliance in IRS e-file programs

All owners of a firm must pass the suitability check before an application will be accepted into IRS e-file.

After the IRS suitability check is completed satisfactorily, you will be issued a letter with information on how you can start to transmit e-filed return data during the filing season. The IRS will send you an e-file marketing/ promotional kit that entitles you to identify yourself as an "Authorized IRS e-file Provider."

Ethical Responsibilities of Paid Tax Preparers

There are numerous ethical and professional standards by which paid tax preparers must abide. Taxpayers are legally responsible for what's on their own tax returns even if prepared by someone else, but tax preparers can also be subject to numerous penalties, and can even be charged with a criminal offense if it is proved that they have knowingly committed tax fraud.

Examples of improper actions by unscrupulous preparers include the preparation and filing of false paper or electronic income tax returns that claim inflated personal or business expenses, false deductions, unallowable credits, or excessive exemptions.   Other legal requirements for paid tax preparers include:

- Signing the return and filling in the preparer areas of the form.
- Giving the client a copy of the return.
- Not charging a contingent fee (percentage of a client's refund) for preparing an original tax return.
- Returning original documents to the client, regardless of any fee dispute.

Anyone who is thinking about offering tax services should read IRS **Circular 230**, *Regulations Governing the Practice of Attorneys, Certified Public Accountants, Enrolled Agents, Enrolled Actuaries, and Appraisers before the Internal Revenue Service.*

"It's important for taxpayers to find qualified tax professionals if they need help preparing and filing their tax returns. Unqualified tax preparers may overlook legitimate deductions or credits that could cause clients to pay more tax than they should. Unqualified preparers may also make costly mistakes causing their clients to incur assessed deficiencies, penalties, and interest. Tax evasion is both risky and a crime, punishable by up to five years imprisonment and a $250,000 fine."

-Melaney J. Partner, IRS Manager

Staying Up To Date

Tax preparers need to keep their continuing education up to date. Tax law changes every year, and even if your state does not have any requirements for tax preparers, it's important to invest in continuing education every year in order to remain current.

Educational Requirements for California Tax Preparers

Becoming a registered tax preparer in California is relatively easy, if you take the time to take a course and keep up with a small continuing education requirement every year. Even if you only have a few tax clients, the cost of registration will pay for itself with your first tax return.

The educational requirements and registration of tax preparers in California is regulated by the California Tax Education Council (CTEC). CTEC was established by the California State Legislature to promote competent tax preparation.

A CTEC registered tax preparer is registered with the state of California to prepare tax returns. CTEC preparers can prepare any type of federal or California tax return, such as tax returns for individuals, partnerships, corporations, estates, and trusts. To earn your CTEC registration, you must complete an approved sixty hour course on individual income taxation. The course must include a minimum of forty-five hours of federal hours and fifteen hours of California material.

Steps to Become a CRTP (California Registered Tax Preparer)
- Successfully complete a CTEC-approved, 60-hour qualifying tax course.
- Obtain a $5,000 tax preparer bond (these are available online for about $25).
- Obtain a certificate of completion from CTEC by completing the CTEC application and submitting with a $25 application fee.

After taking the 60-hour course, you can complete all the other steps online. The whole process should cost less than $300, which you will make back the first time you prepare a tax return. Once you become a registered tax preparer in California, you must complete twenty hours (sixteen federal, four state) of continuing education every year. Continuing education requirements can usually be completed online affordably. There is at least one continuing education provider that offers a yearly renewal CTEC continuation course for less than 20 dollars.

You can find out more about becoming a CRTP at *www.crtc.org*.

Educational Requirements for Oregon Tax Preparers

All persons in Oregon who prepare personal income tax returns for a fee must be licensed. The educational requirements and registration of tax preparers in Oregon is regulated by the Oregon Board of Tax Practitioners. There are two types of licensed tax preparers in Oregon.

The Oregon Tax Board issues two types of licenses. The *Licensed Tax Preparer* is an apprenticeship license that enables a person to lawfully prepare personal income tax returns in Oregon under the supervision of a *Licensed Tax **Consultant***.

The Licensed Tax Consultant is a higher competency license obtained through testing and experience to the point that a licensee may prepare taxes as a self-employed, independent or supervising tax practitioner. In Oregon, a Licensed Tax Preparer must work under the supervision of a Licensed Tax Consultant, a Certified Public Accountant, or an Attorney who prepares tax returns for their clients.

In Oregon, a tax preparer must obtain a license before preparing tax returns for a fee. A Tax Consultant license enables a person to lawfully prepare personal income tax returns in Oregon for a fee as a self-employed or independent tax practitioner.

To become a Licensed Tax Preparer in Oregon:

- You must be at least 18 years of age.
- You must be a high school graduate or have passed an equivalency examination.
- You must complete a minimum of eighty clock hours of basic income tax law education. A course designed specifically for this purpose is offered statewide by community colleges, vocational schools, and approved basic course sponsors.
- You must pass the tax preparer examination administered by the Board with a 75 percent pass rate or higher.

A Licensed Tax Preparer may qualify to take the consultant examination after working a minimum of 780 hours during at least two of the last five years in the capacity of a tax preparer. You can find out more information about obtaining an Oregon tax preparer license at *www.oregon.gov/OTPB*.

Becoming an Enrolled Agent (EA)

An "Enrolled Agent" (EA) is a tax professional who has passed an IRS test covering all aspects of taxation, plus has also passed an IRS background check. An Enrolled Agent has earned the privilege of practicing—representing taxpayers—before the Internal Revenue Service. You do not need a college degree in order to become an Enrolled Agent.

Enrolled Agents, like attorneys and Certified Public Accountants (CPAs), are unrestricted as to which taxpayers they can represent, what types of tax matters they can handle, and which IRS offices they can practice before.

Once you have some experience, you may decide that you may want to become an Enrolled Agent yourself. Becoming an EA will allow you to charge more for tax preparation and other financil services. Enrolled Agents are allowed to represent taxpayers in all administrative levels of the IRS— they can represent taxpayers during the audit process, prepare all types of tax returns, and negotiate with the IRS collections department. Enrolled Agents advise, represent, and prepare tax returns for individuals, partnerships, corporations, estates, trusts, and any entities with tax-reporting requirements.

Only Enrolled Agents are required to demonstrate to the IRS their competence in matters of taxation before they may represent a taxpayer before the IRS. Unlike attorneys and CPAs, who may or may not choose to specialize in taxation, all Enrolled Agents specialize in taxation. Enrolled Agents are the only taxpayer representatives who receive their right to practice from the U.S. government.

The EA license is earned in one of two ways: by passing a comprehensive examination that covers all aspects of the tax code, or by having worked at the IRS for five years in a position that regularly interpreted and applied the tax code and its regulations. All candidates are subjected to a rigorous background check conducted by the IRS. In addition to the EA Exam and application process, the IRS requires Enrolled Agents to complete seventy-two hours of continuing professional education every three years to maintain their Enrolled Agent status.

Steps to Become an Enrolled Agent (EA)

1. Learn! Take a good EA Exam study course and gather information about the Special Enrollment Examination. You will want to download the "Enrolled Agent Candidate Information Bulletin" from the Prometric site *(www. Prometric.com).*

2. Sign up with Prometric to take the Special Enrollment Examination. The easiest way is to sign up online using IRS **Form 2587** on the Prometric/IRS website. The fee to take the exam is $97 for each of the three parts of the exam. Choose a testing site that's convenient for you.

3. Adopt a study plan that covers all the tax topics on the Special Enrollment Examination. Approach each study unit at a pace of three to four hours each.

4. Don't forget your ID! On test day, don't forget your driver's license, passport, or other identification. Arrive early to your test site, sign in, and get situated. During the test, do not speak with other students, or you may be asked to leave the testing center. That section of the test is over, and nothing you say or do now will change your score.

5. Congratulations! You passed! Now you must begin the process of applying for your EA through the IRS. Submit your paperwork and the IRS will review your prior year returns (if applicable) and issue you a Treasury Card.

You do not have to have a degree to take the Enrolled Agent exam, which makes the designation attractive to financial professionals who do not have the time to go back to school, but still want the respect and flexibility that this license will offer.

If you decide that you want to become an Enrolled Agent, there are resources and course information at the end of this volume. Go to *www.enrolledagentreview.com* to get more information. You should also go to the Prometric website and download the EA candidate bulletin to find out everything you need to sign up for the exam. You can find the bulletin at *www.prometric.com/IRS/default.htm.*

Chapter 8: Common Questions and Mistakes to Avoid

One of the biggest hurdles for home-based entrepreneurs is maintaining a professional business atmosphere. The client's perception is imperative to your success. You must carry on your activities in a businesslike manner. This includes avoiding billing errors, practicing excellent customer service, and always maintaining a professional demeanor.

Here are some tips to help you avoid some common beginner blunders:

1. Avoid Bad Clients!

As a financial professional, you need to have honesty and integrity in order to be successful. You should also look for clients that share these qualities. If a client asks you to hide income or cheat on payroll tax returns, it's in your best interest to discontinue your relationship with the client.

Don't compromise your integrity. A client that asks you to do something questionable will have no qualms about not paying his or her bill! A cheating client will eventually cheat you too.

From the very beginning, be choosy. Trust your instincts because they're usually right. If you feel that a client will not pay his or her bill, ask for a retainer in advance. Give your clients a class rating of "A," "B," or "C." Your "A" clients pay on time, send referrals, and listen to your advice. "B" clients may pay a little slower or have other issues. Your "C" clients resist paying their bills and always have money problems, either from mismanagement or downright stupidity. By eliminating your "C" clients, you can have more hours and resources to dedicate to your best clients and also to find more "A" clients.

Even in the beginning, resist accepting clients who are low-level or have the possibility of being slow-payers. Set high standards for yourself and your client base and you'll rarely need to suffer through the hassle of collections. Aim high from the start and you won't be scrambling to get paid over the long term.

2. Give Personal Attention

Give personal attention to your best clients—they are the ones who are going to generate the best referrals. Notice that successful businesspeople tend to travel in the same circles. Provide personalized and frequent contact with the best clients. Slow-pay clients are often the neediest! Train yourself to set firm boundaries with difficult clients right away. It will save you a lot of headaches.

Allow yourself some flexibility. Don't rush from one client site to another. It will just make your job more difficult and clients will sense that you're rushed. Don't make the mistake of scheduling every available minute of your day. Save some time for breaks, lunch, and some extra time for unforeseen tasks.

3. Monitor Your Time

Monitor how you manage your time. Make sure you don't make the mistake of underestimating your time spent on a project. Most professionals are guilty of this. Don't quote your client an estimate of five billable hours and then spend ten hours doing the work! This is a recipe for frustration, and you will end up resenting the client. It is your responsibility to give a client a reasonable estimate for your time.

It is always better to overestimate the cost of services to a client. Clients will be happy if you bill them less than the quoted amount, but they will be very unhappy if you bill them over your quoted price! Remember, clients hate surprises. Make sure that you bill your time honestly and efficiently; your clients will thank you for it, and you'll be much happier if you're not performing your services for free.

Communicate Intelligently!

Provide clients with clear financial information on a regular basis; they will be thankful for the updates. Always communicate clearly about your fees; clients hate surprises more than they hate bills! Point out any additional work that may generate a higher bill.

Even the best clients have high communication needs at times. Create a system that allows you to communicate with your clients on a regular schedule that does not interrupt your work-flow throughout the day. Nothing is more counterproductive to getting work done than answering e-mails constantly. If necessary, set all your calls to voice-mail so you can finish your work in a timely manner. Remember, bookkeeping is not heart surgery. No one is going to die if you don't get them a report right away.

How to Avoid Non-Paying Clients

The best way to avoid payment problems is to avoid problem clients. Learn to recognize warning signs of a bad client choice:

- How long have they been in business? Most businesses fail in the early years, so the longer a firm is in business, the better the chances of receiving timely payments.
- Do they want to haggle with price? If a client complains that your rates are too high, he or she either doesn't value what you do or is strapped for cash.
- Does the prospective client want you to do work with an unreasonable deadline? Those who want their books put in order because of an impending tax deadline, or who haven't paid taxes for several years and now need you to help them get their act together because the IRS is chasing them are bad news. They likely don't handle their other obligations on time either.

Don't be afraid to "fire" a client who is repeatedly slow about paying his or her bill. You are wasting precious energy on a difficult client who may stop paying you altogether.

Remember, your time is valuable, too. Every hour you dedicate to a client that requires lots of unbillable handholding or who doesn't pay your invoice becomes lost money in your pocket. Instead, you could be searching for a better client who values your services and is a joy to work with.

Take your pick as to which kind you want. You do have a choice.

Helpful Hints on Billing

On your bill, recap the work you did for the client. Don't add up items. Just include a one paragraph description, such as:

"Bookkeeping services rendered for October, payroll services, and bank reconciliations."

Avoid charging for small items, such as photocopying, unless costs exceed $20. Small petty charges infuriate clients, and they're counter-productive to your success. Customers like stability and consistency.

No one likes paying bills, so don't give anyone an excuse to get annoyed. Make sure that you date your bills on the last day of the month for which you provided services. For example, for your October bill, date it October 31. Don't date the bill November 1 because your client needs to know that the services and the bill are for the same month.

Avoiding the Dreaded IRS "Trust Fund Recovery" Penalty

Did you know that you could become responsible for a client's unpaid taxes? It's true! It's called the "Trust Fund Recovery" penalty, and it is the most dreaded penalty in the IRS's arsenal. Why? Because the penalty is 100 percent of the taxes due—yes, that's right. A 100 percent penalty! Plus, it can be assessed against employees, bookkeepers, and other members of a company.

Here's how the penalty happens: An employer is responsible for withholding federal and state taxes, but the employee to whom withholding is delegated could be held personally liable for monies withheld if the amounts are not paid. Personal liability for the taxes can be imposed upon the person "responsible" for paying them to the government, including, in certain cases, a bookkeeper or payroll clerk.

Internal Revenue Code (IRC) Sec. 6672(a), referred to as the "100 percent penalty," is used to recover employer payroll taxes from bookkeepers responsible for withholding and paying them. Even check-signing authority not involving payroll or payroll taxes can trigger personal liability if the signer's job includes paying creditors, and tax authorities deem that such funds "came from" payroll taxes withheld and therefore "belong" to them.

If the IRS thinks it can't recover from a firm, it may sue the employee. The IRS may even sue the employee before or instead of attempting to recover from the firm because anyone responsible for withholding and paying taxes is as liable as the employer.

If income, Social Security, and Medicare taxes that a business withholds from employee wages are not deposited or paid to the IRS, the trust fund recovery penalty may apply. The penalty is the full amount of the unpaid trust fund tax. This penalty may apply to you if these unpaid taxes cannot be immediately collected from the business.

Trust Fund Recovery Penalty Horror Story

Jake[7] was a supervisor at Barnaby Windows Corporation. His boss, Stanley, ran a very successful business and grossed over $7 million in sales annually. The business had twelve full-time employees as well as a number of independent contractors. Everything was going fine until late 2006 when Stanley's wife passed away from a sudden heart attack.

Stanley began acting erratically and developed a drug problem. Jake ran the office as best as he could, and since he had check-signing privileges to the bank account, he signed the employees' paychecks until money ran out in late 2007. After that, the business closed and Stanley disappeared. Jake found another job quickly and began working as a supervisor for another contractor. Everything was going great until the IRS showed up at his workplace. The IRS revenue agent confirmed that Jake had check-signing privileges at Barnaby Windows Corporation, his former employer, and told him he would be fully responsible for the unpaid payroll taxes that Stanley failed to pay in 2006 and 2007.

"But wait!" cried Jake, "I just did the best I could—I never stole any money—I just signed the employee paychecks!"

"Too bad," said the IRS, "You knew (or should have known) that the payroll taxes were not being remitted to the IRS. According to the law, that makes you responsible."

The trust fund recovery penalty may be imposed on all persons who are "determined by the IRS" to be responsible for collecting, accounting for, and paying these taxes, and who acted willfully in not doing so. A responsible person can be an officer or employee of a corporation, an accountant, or even a volunteer director. A responsible person also may include one who signs checks for the corporation or otherwise has authority to cause the spending of business funds (IRC Section 6672).

Solution: Don't be the only signature on checks. Authority to sign a check represents authority to disburse funds and can trigger personal liability if withheld taxes are not paid. You are protected against the liability of "final authority" if your firm requires that all checks have a second signature of a supervisor or corporate officer after you have signed it.

Note: If you have to sign paychecks, temporarily (an owner is out of town) or permanently (you are at a remote location), your only protection may be to have your employer give someone else "final authority." This tip comes from AIPB's *The Bookkeeper's Guide to Internal Controls.*

Finally, if you find out that your client or employer is intentionally NOT paying payroll taxes but still withholding them from employees, you should seriously consider immediately breaking the engagement with the client. Even if you are completely innocent, do you really want the IRS beating down your door because your client refused to pay his payroll taxes? It's just not worth the risk. You should send a certified letter ending the engagement with the client as soon as it is feasible for you to do so.

Recordkeeping Requirements for Employers

The IRS has very specific recordkeeping requirements for employers. You should understand these and make sure that your client is aware of them. Businesses are required to keep permanent books of account or records that are sufficient to establish the amount of gross income and deductions, credits, and other matters shown on a tax return. The IRS will accept any form of journal, whether it is a complex software-based accounting system or just a cheap spiral notebook showing income and expenses.

The business must keep backup records (receipts, invoices, and packing slips) in order to substantiate the income and expenses reported on its tax returns. Taxpayers are required to substantiate business deductions for travel and entertainment expenses. Substantiation of who, when, where, why, and how much is generally required.

Employment and payroll records must be kept available at all times for inspection by IRS officers and designated employees and must be retained as long as they may be material.

Since the IRS generally has three years from the date a return was due or filed or two years from the date the tax was paid (whichever is later) to assess tax, a business must retain all records and forms until the later time. Records relating to a claim for a loss from worthless securities should be kept for seven years.

Keep all records of employment taxes for at least four years. These should be available for IRS review. Employer records should include:
- Employer Identification Number (EIN)
- Amounts and dates of all wage, annuity, and pension payments
- Amounts of tips reported by employees
- Records of allocated tips
- The Fair Market Value of in-kind wages paid
- Names, addresses, Social Security numbers, and occupations of employees and recipients
- Any employee copies of Forms W-2 and W-2c that were returned to you as undeliverable
- Dates of employment for each employee
- Periods for which employees and recipients were paid while absent due to sickness or injury and the amount and weekly rate of payments you or third-party payers made to them
- Copies of employees' and recipients' income tax withholding allowance certificates (Forms W-4, W-4P, W-4S, and W-4V)
- Dates and amounts of tax deposits made and acknowledgment numbers for deposits made by EFTPS
- Copies of returns filed
- Records of fringe benefits and expense reimbursements provided to employees, including substantiation

Source: **www.IRS.gov**; *The Internal Revenue Service, US Department of the Treasury*

What Happens When I Become Successful and Want to Grow?

A lot of freelance bookkeepers and tax professionals wonder how long it might take to become financially independent. For many freelancers it can take about three to five years, give or take.

That doesn't mean that you will be struggling for five years, it just means that on average, that's how long it might take you to establish a good solid client base.

The amount of work one person can accomplish is finite. So how can a successful business owner cope with overload and still continue to grow the company? There are generally only two viable choices:

1.   Raise rates so that there are fewer clients who will pay higher rates.
2.   Get help to carry some of the workload.

Although in theory the sky can be the limit when it comes to the rates charged by a one-person business, a bookkeeping and tax services company has better chances at long-term profitability and stability if its prosperity depends on more than one person.

When it comes to getting help, the traditional route for most businesses is to hire employees. In the bookkeeping industry, hiring freelancers, also known as subcontractors, has become commonplace. Some bookkeeping is now even being outsourced to India by quite a few accounting firms!

Hiring a subcontractor yourself can be a more profitable choice, especially in the early, financially challenging stages of business growth. There are, of course, companies in the industry who continue to use a combination of employees and subcontractors to handle the inherent fluctuating workload, with good success.

Why Subcontractors Rather than Employees?

With subcontractors there is an "easy come, easy go" advantage when it comes to a variable workload. If you're entrenched in the common feast-or-famine cycle, subcontractors will save your neck when you're inundated with multiple projects all at the same time. Unlike employees, however, "subs" won't cost you a dime when work is lean. Subcontractors are there when you need them and not a burden when you don't. You pay only for productive time or output produced. Bottom line: You pay only for what you get, no more.

The funny thing about hiring subcontractors is that all of their advantages to you and your business are the same advantages you're selling to your own clients for using your services–outsourcing at its best!

Don't Disguise Employees as Subcontractors

On the other hand (the one with the wallet), employees cost a lot of money, especially if you try to call them subcontractors and the IRS disagrees with you! It is very important that you are absolutely clear on the differences between employees and subcontractors. If you hire an independent bookkeeper to handle some of your workload, and he or she also has other clients, that person is probably an independent contractor. But if he or she only does work for you and no one else, and has no intention of doing work for anyone else, you may have a problem.

If you hire employees, you generally need to withhold income taxes, pay half of the Social Security and Medicare taxes, and pay unemployment tax on wages to both state and federal agencies. In contrast, however, an employer generally does not have to withhold or pay any taxes on payments to independent contractors. It is easy to see why many companies try to label some of their employees as subcontractors. But beware:

> "If you classify an employee as an independent contractor and you have no reasonable basis for doing so," says Uncle Sam, "you may be held liable for employment taxes for that worker."

Ouch!

Finding Subcontractors

So where can legal subcontractors be found? The bad news is that they are not necessarily easy to find. Often, you will find them via word of mouth, since many work from home and don't list their services in the telephone book. You may have good luck finding subcontractors on Craigslist (*www.Craigslist.org*).

Other sites are more general in their focus, geared more toward independent contracting for self-employed individuals of a variety of professions, from consultants to accountants and everything in between, including business support services. (A couple of examples are www.elance.com and www.allfreelance.com.) Another option is to spend some time running a search at one of the major search engine sites (Yahoo or Google, for example). After a little sifting through your search results, you will find websites galore that will lead to subcontractor candidate possibilities. Some of these sites will allow you to list your needs and have subs contact you.

The Pay-Rate Tango

If you've never hired subcontractors, the burning question might be, "How much should I pay them?" or "Can I afford to pay a subcontractor's rates?"

The former question is probably more practical than the latter. The reality is that most subcontractors will wait for you to tell them how much you will pay, despite the fact that they are in business for themselves. If you brought a large copying and binding job down to Kinko's, you wouldn't expect the counter person to ask you how much you want to pay to get the job done. However, it is common in the business support field for subcontractors to expect you to suggest how much will be paid to perform a project.

There are several different angles to consider when it comes to setting the price on your outsourced work. As you gain experience in working with subcontractors, the goal is a win-win situation for each of you, that is, if you expect to have people you can count on when you need them most.

So what is a fair price to pay your subcontractors? One method is to pay the subcontractor based on a flat fee for each project. You can figure the price as though you were going to do the job in-house.

Add a little extra for unexpected problems. Then agree to pay the subcontractor anywhere from one-half to two-thirds of the total, whatever seems to be a fair price for the work and deadline involved. Your cut of the job will depend on the time necessary to oversee and package the final product for your client.

The difference between what you pay your subcontractor and what you charge your client should be enough to cover your time to manage and deliver the project, with a little left over as profit. There really is no single "right" answer when it comes to working out a pricing schedule between you and your subcontractors.

No matter which method you choose, whether it is one of the above or another negotiated compromise, be sure that both you and your subcontractor will benefit from the working arrangement. Experience is ultimately the best teacher here. Establishing a price that works is often much like dancing; as long as you don't step on each other's toes, it can be a pleasant experience.

Once you have come to a verbal agreement with your subcontractor, it is time to turn it into a professional working relationship with a written contract. This book includes a sample contract that can modified for your use.

Chapter 9: How to Manage Your Cash Flow

We all need cash in our pocket to buy our daily needs and pay our bills. In business it is no different. Without good cash flow, any business will come to a sudden, screeching halt without the cash to pay vendors, meet payroll, buy essential supplies, or to pay taxes when due.

Cash flow can be an indicator of your business's health, but it is not the same as profit. A failing business with good cash flow can still stay afloat, at least temporarily, even though it may be losing a great deal of money from its bottom line.

Of course, a healthy business that is run well, with a decent profit margin, is likely to enjoy adequate cash flow AND a nice bottom line. But sooner or later, for whatever reason, most small businesses face some kind of a cash flow crunch, at least temporarily. Sometimes this happens right after you make a big change, such as a move *out* of a home office to a permanent office location.

In **Part One** of this section you'll learn about strategies that will pull in the cash, many of which may already be available to you. Some of these methods will yield a burst of new income, while others should be used as strategies that will increase your cash flow over the long haul.

In **Part Two** you'll concentrate on strategies that will help you hold onto your earnings and stretch it further. You work hard for your money, and in turn, these methods will make your money work hard for you. Again, some of these methods will give you dramatic, quick results. But most of them will make your business stronger for the long term, if used consistently. Both types of cash flow methods are important if you want to build a truly successful business.

Part Three is where you can pick and choose which strategies work best for you. This section is designed to be used over and over again while building and perfecting your very own cash flow system. You can photocopy the worksheets we have provided and make your own projections.

To really make your system work, you will need focus and a willingness to do things differently if you've already been in business for awhile. After all, you can't expect new results if you keep running your business the same way you've always run it.

Part I: Cash Flow Generation

Part II: Cash Flow Savings

Part III: Your Own Cash Flow Plan

Part I – Cash Flow Generation

When your business hits a dry spell and the cash dries up, it can cause rough operations that make your business sputter and grind to a halt. Everything becomes more difficult. Let's make sure that never happens in your business.

Use as many strategies as you can in a short period of time. That will give you a quick boost, as well as lay the foundation for backup systems so that you will never hit dry cash flow again.

Eight Strategies to Get Paid Quickly!

1. Invoice Promptly

As strange as it seems, it is not uncommon for small service business owners to feel uncomfortable about asking to be paid! If you run a service business, and you don't collect payment when services are rendered (which might be part of the reason for a cash crunch in the first place), your clients may quickly forget that they owe you.

The longer you wait to bill your clients, the less likely it is they will remember how much they loved your work and pay you promptly. If you are slow to send your invoices, they may also conclude that you do not expect quick payment and will take their time in sending their money.

We suggest that you present your invoices at the time services are delivered, if at all possible. Sending your invoice by e-mail speeds the process up even more. If issuing invoices immediately is not practical in your business, be sure to issue your invoices weekly, or at least twice per month on designated days, such as on the fifteenth and the last day of each month. It's a habit worth forming. Invoice quickly and invoice often.

2. Send Monthly Statements Regularly

Statements should be sent out on the same day of the month each and every month. That makes for steady cash flow because it reminds clients that they still owe you and lets them know that you are not going to forget about it either.

And, of course, the easiest way to keep up with your invoicing and sending statements on a regular basis is to have a good bookkeeping system. Set reminders in your bookkeeping program so that the process is as automated as possible. If you're still keeping your financial records on paper or using an Excel spreadsheet, you are shooting yourself in the foot. That's because you must create all your invoices and statements manually. If you're in this situation, seriously consider using at least the free version of QuickBooks (Simple Start) which is designed for startup businesses. It is very easy to use and is fully functional.

The catch with the Simple Start version is that you can't have more than 20 clients and/or vendors. Once you reach that threshold, you must bite the bullet and buy the software. But by then, your cash will be flowing and you will be well on your way to using your time for generating income – not just collecting for the work you've already done.

Bottom line: You want to send statements of outstanding balances to your clients on a regular basis and QuickBooks software is the best way because it is easy to use and saves you precious time.

3. Don't Be Patient

Of course, you may occasionally have a few clients who, despite prompt billing and statement reminders, are s-l-o-w in paying your bills. (We have some additional suggestions for dealing with them later.) A fast and effective way to give them a nudge to clear their balance is to do one of these:

Pick up the phone and give slow-paying clients a call. This doesn't need to be an unpleasant task. It can be a friendly call to check in and see how they're doing. You may actually pick up new work, simply because of initiating contact! But in the course of your chat, do not forget to ask about the "status" of the invoice.

Send a statement and/or copy of the invoice with a colorful collection sticker to gently (or not so gently) remind them it's time to pay. Collection stickers can be found online that are inexpensive and quite effective.

Combine these two strategies for maximum effectiveness. Send the bill or statement with a collection sticker to get their attention. Then follow up with a call regarding the status of the outstanding balance a week to ten days later.

Ask and you shall receive. It is one of the best ways to bring in a good deal of cash quickly. You've done the work, you deserve to be paid!

4. Accept Credit Cards

It's amazing how many service businesses still do not accept payments by credit card. Accepting credit cards allows you to receive client payments immediately into your bank account – which is a big advantage – AND you will also attract clients who might not otherwise do business with you. That means increased revenues. Accepting credit cards adds to the professionalism of your business.

If you work with your clients face-to-face and want to physically accept their credit card payments, you will need to get a merchant account. That can actually drain your cash flow in the beginning because there's usually a hefty setup fee, monthly fees, as well as a fee that is a percentage of each sale you pull in by credit card. In our opinion, unless you're running a large volume product-based operation, that's too expensive to make good sense.

That's why we suggest using PayPal. Your clients do not need to have a PayPal account to pay you, but if they do, it is a very easy way for them to pay off their balance owed using either a credit card or direct online payment from their checking account. Additionally, you can invoice your clients online using PayPal's invoicing feature. It is fast, secure, and free to set up.

If you already have a PayPal account, the fastest way you can make this strategy work for you is to add a notation on your invoices that says:

"We Accept Payment Online and by Credit Card through PayPal"

And then list your PayPal e-mail address. Any clients that already use PayPal will know what to do. I (Gabrielle) have used this method with excellent results. It's a great feeling to open your e-mail and see messages informing you that money has been deposited instantly into your account. Try it!

5. Progress Bill Large Projects

On large projects that may span over several months, consider billing on a progress basis or in intervals. This avoids sending a huge bill that the client may have difficulty paying all at once upon the completion of the project. It also helps to even out your cash flow to bill in smaller portions throughout the course of the project.

We suggest, however, that you pass this idea by your client before sending out your invoice, or include it in your job proposal right from the start. Clear communication of your intention to ease cash flow pressure on the both of you will avoid any unnecessary misunderstandings or disputes. Think win-win.

6. Prioritize Projects that are Nearly Complete

Once you have collected the vast majority of your Accounts Receivable balances, the next fastest way to get money in the door is to focus on, and finish, any projects that are nearly complete. The sooner you finish them, the sooner you can issue the invoices and get paid.

This may take a bit of time management on your part, especially if your day is filled with many distractions. You'll need to take charge! Block out concentrated, uninterrupted time for these projects on your calendar a week at a time. Plan no more than two or three projects per day. And keep these appointments as if you were meeting with those clients face to face. If you want to bring in the cash, you need to focus and be productive. Think green, and it will get done!

Another anti-procrastination tactic that I (Gabrielle) have used with success is to call or e-mail each of these clients whose projects I am working on and to announce to them exactly when their work will be completed. By doing this, I not only risk a continued cash crunch if I put off getting the work done, but I also risk my reputation with my clients! Higher stakes mean higher productivity. Try it! You'll see that it does help to get you focused and moving quickly. And the sooner each project is completed, the sooner it can be billed and paid. That's the stuff cash flow is made of!

7. Require Deposits Up Front

If you have more than your fair share of slow-paying clients, or worse yet, clients who never pay you at all, it's time to start weeding out those who don't appreciate your work from those who do. These are the ones who are probably major contributors to your cash crunches in the first place! This method will cause them to pay up or get out.

Start telling your clients that you now require a signed Work Order with a deposit on every new project. Charge a 25 percent to 50 percent deposit. By doing so, you will actually raise your clients' perception of your professionalism and repel those who aren't serious about paying for your work in a timely fashion. Of course, you may choose to apply this new rule to only your slow-paying clients if your cash is not strapped too tightly. And don't let the fear of losing these deadbeat clients stop you. If they do not accept your new terms, let them go. By doing so, you will clear the way for new, fast-paying clients who will take less time and effort to service.

My clients who have had the faith and courage to firmly follow this advice are surprised by the quick and dramatic impact it has had on increasing their cash flow. They are amazed at how this one simple shift in how they do business attracts higher quality, prompt-paying clients while the deadbeats go away.

8. Raise Your Rates
You are probably undercharging for your services and you've got a cash crunch to show for it!
An excellent way to know what you should be charging is to check out your competition. This can be done through the Internet or by calling and simply asking competitors their rates on specific services. If you are shy about doing that, have a friend do it for you. You could even tell them that you are doing market research – which you are!

If you discover that you're not charging at least a middle-of-the-road rate, your rates are too low! Your industry association may also have information on standard rates for the services you provide. And even if you're charging a fair rate, nudge up your rates by at least 10 percent if you haven't raised your rates in awhile. That's just normal business procedure. The easiest way to raise your rates is with new clients. But if you have several clients who are usually more trouble than they're worth, the next time they come through the door, be sure to apply your new rates to them as well!

Go To Where the Clients Are

Here is a short list of the most popular sites where you can very quickly find paying contract jobs, and with a little time, build up your regular client base:

www.craigslist.org – This site serves as a mostly free online classified advertiser. You will probably want to start with the site that is for the major city closest to you, but you can search any of the pages. Use the Jobs section to find contract positions for the services you provide. You can also list a free ad for your services here.

www.elance.com – You can post your profile as a service provider for free, but if you wish to actively bid on available contract jobs, you will have to join as a paying member. There are different membership levels, with the lowest being affordable on a monthly basis.

www.guru.com – Similar to elance.com, this site has a free basic membership, however you can bid on jobs if you agree to pay a higher referral fee. If you upgrade, your membership fees are most reasonable if paid on a yearly basis.

Toot Your Own Horn and Get Free Publicity for your Business!

It's not difficult to get some free publicity. And when you do get it, you'll likely get a short term burst of new business inquiries, and in some cases, it can also fuel long-term traffic to your website. In turn, that will give you a steady trickle of new business inquiries as well. Here are a few of the best methods we know of for getting free publicity:

Be a guest speaker or do a free seminar for your Chamber of Commerce or other local small business or industry organizations. If you're the outgoing type, this will give you valuable visibility as an expert in your community. If you offer complementing informational products to attendees, you can also get paid for your efforts, as well as build your list of prospects.

Write up a press release for any new services you are offering, or any other newsworthy happenings within your business that may be of interest to your target market. Doing charity work or donating your services to community efforts will also get your name into the public eye – if you let the press know about it. Press releases may not cause a sudden cash surge in your business, but it will support long-term recognition of you and your business, supporting long-term business growth.

Write articles for online or offline publication. Editors of local weekly newspapers, trade journals and online newsletters are hungry for useful content. Write brief, 300-800 word articles on subjects surrounding your expertise. Then offer them as free content to editors on a regular basis. You will build your credibility and be pulling more traffic to your website immediately. Be sure to include in all of your articles a bio or resource box which mentions your services and gives a link to your website.

Strategies to Find Extra Cash in a Hurry

Clean Up and Get Paid For It!

When you're in a real tight pinch for cash, it's a great time to uncover and liquidate the hidden assets in your business. We're talking about everything you have of value in your business that is not currently contributing to your bottom line. Consider it spring cleaning time for your business. Do you have some old equipment kicking around that still works, but you're not using anymore? Do you have old books or training materials that you just never got around to using?

Why not clean out and turn these items into cash? You can do this easily by selling these items online. Here are some of the best sites we've found for selling what you don't need quickly and cheaply:

www.ebay.com – This is the most popular auction site on the Web. You can sell pretty much anything you want here. It takes a bit of time to set up your sales pages, especially when you're learning in the beginning, but the fees are low, and you can re-run your ads over and over if your items don't sell at first. HOT TIP: Make sure your auctions end on a Sunday. That is when most of the rabid eBay shoppers do most of their buying.

www.amazon.com – Amazon is best known as a bookseller. And of course you can sell your used books quite easily here. But you can also sell any other items they carry, if you have the same exact item (in new or used condition) for sale. This is an easy way to sell at the price you want. You do not have to set up your own sales page, since Amazon provides all the product pictures and written details about your items. However, Amazon also allows you to sell your item as an auction, if you wish.

www.half.com – This is eBay's answer to Amazon. You can sell your used books here almost the same way as you would on Amazon. In fact, you can list the same books simultaneously on both sites for better exposure.

www.craigslist.org – This is a good site to use if you have large furniture items or equipment that would be too costly to ship and you need to reach a local market. The ads are free, so you won't have to pay any fees on your sales either.

Part Two – Cash Flow Savings

Money is a funny thing. It seems that the more we have, the more we spend. If you find that much of your cash is going out just as fast, or even faster, than it's coming in, it might be time to implement some cash preserving strategies.

By plugging up some of the holes in your cash reservoir, the money coming into your business will be more closely watched and have the job of working harder for you. Getting into the habit of holding onto your money longer will automatically boost your available cash without the need to work harder or pull in lots of new clients.

Four Strategies for Getting More With Less

1. Don't Pay Your Bills Early

If you're one of those people who pays bills as soon as they come in, stop it! You are probably wasting time doing more administrative work than you need to, and you're strapping your cash flow in the process. Instead, schedule your bill paying for only once, or at most, twice per month. You can still pay your bills on time while preserving your cash until you really need to let it go.

A great way to make sure no bills get forgotten is to use the Enter Bills and Pay Bills functions in QuickBooks. Then use the Reminders and/or your To Do List (also in QuickBooks). You will be notified when it's time to pay your bills with the least amount of effort and minimum drain on your cash flow.

2. Reduce Your Overhead

Periodically run your Profit & Loss report and review your expenses. Look specifically at the bills you're paying every month, quarterly, or annually. Does the amount you're paying out contribute to a healthy bottom line? Do you still need pay for all those goods or services? Can you get a better price?

Some of the expenses you may want to review regularly and research to see if you can get a better price or decide if you really need them at all are:
- Insurance premiums
- Office and inventory supplies
- Subscriptions and memberships
- Telephone and Internet services
- Advertising and marketing services

You should review your bills at least annually to trim any accumulated fat from your payables. You'll be amazed at how much this simple ritual can save you. Do it on a regular basis for maximum effectiveness.

3. Make Tax-Smart Decisions

In the course of running their businesses, many entrepreneurs never stop to think about taxes when they make decisions about where to set up their office, when to upgrade their equipment, how many business trips to go on, or what health insurance to buy. It doesn't seem relevant at the time. But it can make a big difference come April 15th.

Home Office Done Right – If you have a home-based business, be sure that you have a separate space for it. Measure the space used exclusively and regularly for your business, as well as the square footage of your entire home. This will render a percentage that can be used to arrive at substantial business deductions that will both reduce your income tax and your self-employment tax.

Warning: Do not run your business from your living room table and do not include a play area for your children in your office. While convenient, both of these scenarios will render your home office ineligible to take deductions otherwise available for a home-based business.

Be Healthy and Save Taxes – If you're self-employed and your spouse does not have health insurance coverage available through his or her employer, you may want to consider a High Deductible Health Plan (HDHP) for you and your family. Your premiums will be lower than a traditional health insurance plan, and this type of plan means that you're eligible to also open a Health Savings Account (HSA).

HSAs are special savings accounts where you can make contributions that are tax deductible "above the line" and from which you can withdraw money any time to pay for a wide range of out-of-pocket medical costs tax-free. That includes medical costs that may not covered by your health insurance.

With the combination of an HDHP and an HSA, you get the ability to deduct 100 percent of your healthcare costs, even if you don't itemize your deductions on your tax return. This self-employed tax break gets you a solid medical policy that is good for your health, finances, and your cash flow too.

If you use a credit card that accrues travel points, miles, or cash, pay for your out-of-pocket medical costs using that credit card(instead of your HSA debit car). Then reimburse yourself for your medical costs using either a check or the bill pay function from your HSA account. The payment should be made out to you, indicating that it is a reimbursement of medical expenses paid. Use the money from the HSA account to pay the medical expenses part of your credit card bill. (DO NOT use HSA funds for personal purposes or you will be taxed AND penalized!) After the payments have been made, you will effectively be getting perks on your credit card for free. As with all tax matters, be sure to keep good records of all transactions.

Mix Business with Pleasure - The IRS says the primary purpose of a trip must be for business in order to deduct the expenses. However, you're allowed to spend some time having fun. A trip for business purposes means that the number of days used for business is greater than the days spent having fun. The IRS considers travel days as business days. Every time you go to a continuing education event, or a networking event, use this as an opportunity to have some fun and also get a business deduction.

All your business days' expenses are deductible, including travel, lodging, and meals (although meals are subject to a 50 percent limit). The roundtrip travel costs to and from your destination are also deductible because the trip is primarily for business. Only the expenses incurred during your fun days are not deductible.

Caution: If your trip is NOT primarily for business, that is, if the trip consists of more vacation days than business days, the expenses you can deduct are reduced drastically. There are also special considerations as to whether or not you can deduct expenses for others who accompany you on the trip.

There are many more tax-advantaged decisions you can make throughout the year in your business that will ultimately affect your cash flow. The best strategy here is to plan ahead and discuss your situation with a tax professional.

4. Use Strategic Procrastination

We are constantly barraged with sales messages every day. When it comes to business, sometimes we are sitting ducks for that shiny new electronic gadget or cutting edge online subscription. Many times, the sales tactics work so well that we quickly shell out our hard-earned cash without even thinking about it. We readily believe that this new technology will make our business better. But the reality may be quite different.

Sometimes it may be months or even years before we get around to actually doing anything with that new purchase. Or maybe we never end up using it at all and it collects dust on the shelf. The truth is, we handed over our money and the only thing that happened was a draining of our cash supply.

It's time to slam on the brakes when it comes to blind business purchases and practice a little "strategic procrastination."

Whenever your eye gets caught by something new that promises to benefit your business, consciously procrastinating on the buying process can save you a bundle while salvaging your cash flow. The higher the price tag, the more vigilant you should be about becoming clear on WHEN is the right time to purchase, if at all.

There are several questions to ask yourself, long before you ever reach for your wallet:

Will this new purchase clearly help me move my business more efficiently in the direction I planned THIS YEAR? Or will it distract me into moving in a slightly different direction?

Can I justify the COST of this product? How long will it take to recover that cost?

Do I have another way to accomplish the same purpose cheaper or for free with what I already have right now?

If I can see that this product will significantly help me in the short term, do I really need it RIGHT NOW? Or am I not quite ready to put it to use yet?

WHEN do I really NEED this product? Can it wait a week or a month?

Do I have the TIME in my schedule to devote to learning how to implement this new product right away? If not, when will I have the time?

Once these questions have been answered, save the sales information on the product and set up a task in Outlook to revisit the decision later (or use any type of reminder system you have available to you). Later is usually at least a week or more. If you decide that you definitely do want that new product for your business, but do not need it now, schedule the task to consider it again for purchase (using Outlook, if you have it) for a time when you think you will be ready to implement it immediately.

By using this procedure, you'll be amazed at how long you can put off a purchase, even when it is something you really do need. This system also prevents you from forgetting or losing information about important tools that you can use in your business. And best of all, it prevents you from jumping the gun and draining your cash flow prematurely.

Three Ways to Streamline and Save

1. Prioritize Your Time With a "Must Do" List

If you're like most of us, you generally think you can get a lot more done in a day than you really can. The reality is we can usually only get two, maybe three, important tasks done in a day.

A habit that will make a BIG difference in your cash flow and your bottom line is to begin each day with a clear goal of the two or three (absolutely no more than four) most important tasks you need to accomplish. If you're focused on cash flow, make sure they're tasks that will produce money quickly.

This is a simple but powerful, low-tech way to keep your top daily priorities in focus, no matter how many interruptions you face. This is my own (Gabrielle here) technique for consistently getting done the most important work of my day:

- At the close of the work day, write down three, but no more than four, tasks you MUST get done on the following day. I like to use colored index cards.
- Tape the list to the bottom of your computer screen or some other strategic location where you will see it throughout your day.
- When you arrive at your desk in the morning, immediately tackle one of your "Must Do Tasks" before you do anything else, including reading your e-mail. This creates momentum and starts your day off right.
- Check off each task as it is completed.

Try this every day for a week. You'll be shocked by how much you can get done in a short period of time. Keep it up and your bank account will soon thank you for it too.

2. Minimize Time Out of the Office

By working from your office rather than going out to meet your clients, you can get more work done in less time. You will not waste time on unnecessary travel and you'll be able to move more quickly from one paying project to the next—maximizing your productivity. Use the Internet, fax, e-mail, and telephone whenever possible.

Any necessary errands should be bundled together and scheduled weekly, preferably during non-prime time working hours, so you can do them all at once and in the least amount of time. This too will save you lots of travel time (as well as travel costs) which can be better used to stay focused on income-producing activities.

3. Keep Up With Your Own Books

Keeping your books up to date will increase your cash flow. Not directly--but it *will* help you see where exactly your money is going and help you curb unnecessary spending before it becomes a problem. Timely recordkeeping also helps you to avoid cash-sucking mistakes like double paying bills or paying late fees. Who wants to lose precious cash to unnecessary service charges, penalties, and higher interest rates?

Beyond simple cash flow, keeping your books up to date on at least a monthly, if not a weekly, basis puts you in a position of power. You can keep a close watch on how your business is doing. Which of your products or services are most profitable? What costs are too high? Which area of your business should you expand and develop? Are there some you should nix? And, of course, what is your business really worth? Accurate and up-to-date books will give you answers to all of these questions. Even the best bookkeepers fall behind sometimes, but keeping your books up to date is essential to your success. As the saying goes, time is money, and money is what cash flow is all about.

Part III – Putting It All Together: Create Your Own Cash Flow System

Now that you've had the chance to read through all the cash flow strategies, you probably have a good idea about which ones you'll be putting into practice in your own business and which ones you'll leave behind or at consider at a later date.

You've actually already taken the first vital step in creating a sustainable bookkeeping business! You see, for any system to work, it must include simple, effective actions that can be done consistently. The most effective actions are usually the ones we WANT to do, because we're more likely to keep doing them if they give us good results.

In the beginning, we want (or need) fast results. But fast isn't always best. We also need to use strategies that will build solid STEADY cash flow over the long term. Those strategies protect us like a cash reserve account when, for one reason or another, our bread-and-butter cash sources slow down or even dry up.

To build your own cash-flow strategy, you need to put in place the strategies that will work best for your particular business. To help you do that, listed on the next page are all of the strategies, and they are categorized:

- Cash Generating
- Cash Saving

In building a system that works, you'll want to make sure that you're using strategies from both categories. That's not hard to do since all of the strategies fall into one or the other category. Find the combination that works best for you. Start with only a few strategies and then add at least one new strategy per month.

I also suggest that once you find what's working best for your business, document your procedures and build system maps so they can be duplicated on an ongoing basis by you or anyone else in your organization. Then you can delegate the tasks needed to produce results consistently.

This bonus section includes a Cash Flow System Worksheet for your use. Copy that page and fill in the strategies that you plan to start implementing right away; schedule time on your calendar now to get it going. Then add at least one new strategy per month for sustained cash flow growth. Now you're on your way!

Cash Flow Generation Strategies

All of the strategies on this page will generate an infusion of cash into your business. Pick at least three to implement immediately:

- Invoice promptly
- Send statements regularly
- Don't be patient
- Accept credit cards
- Progress bill large projects
- Prioritize projects that are nearly complete
- Require deposits up front
- Raise your rates
- Generate more business and new referrals from existing clients
- Create a simple website
- Make your presence known on the web
- Go to where the clients are
- Take the initiative to contact inactive clients
- Toot your own horn
- Sell your knowledge
- Clean up and get paid for it

Cash Flow Savings Strategies

All of the strategies on this page will help to keep cash in your business longer. Pick at least two to implement immediately in your business.

- Don't pay your bills early
- Reduce your overhead
- Slash payroll costs
- Make tax-smart decisions
- Use strategic procrastination
- Prioritize your time with a "Must Do" list
- Minimize time out of the office
- Keep up with your own books

Cash Flow System Worksheet

Date: _____

What do you need?
- Immediate cash needed!
- Stop the rollercoaster! I need steady cash flow
- I need some new income streams

How much cash do you need this month? $_____

What's caused the cash crunch? _____

You're on track to make how much this year? $_____

Which strategies will you use?   By when?

1. _____   _____

2. _____   _____

3. _____   _____

Actions needed   Who will take action?

1. _____   _____

2. _____   _____

3. _____   _____

4. _____   _____

5. _____   _____

6. _____   _____

7. _____   _____

8. _____   _____

9. _____   _____

Chapter 10: Case Studies of Success

Now we are going to introduce two successful freelance bookkeepers, Sylvia Jaumann and Mike Sheldon. Both of them are self-employed and have been freelance bookkeepers for many years.

Read their stories and see if your story is similar to theirs. They both share their marketing ideas and their mistakes. Learn from other successful bookkeepers and financial professionals. Learning from others is a great way to avoid errors and get ideas for how to nurture your own bookkeeping business.

Sylvia Jaumann has been a professional bookkeeper for over eighteen years. After several years working as a bookkeeping employee, Sylvia decided to go out on her own and start her own bookkeeping business as she knew that self-employed bookkeepers make more money than employed ones.

But she found the going tough for the first year as she struggled with all the systems needed to run a bookkeeping business. There was literally no information on how to start a bookkeeping business at the time. So she ended up subcontracting for a professional bookkeeper just to make ends meet and learned many tips and tricks to running a bookkeeping business that she didn't know before.

Sylvia took this information and turned it into the "Secrets to Starting & Running Your Own Bookkeeping Business" e-book and "Bookkeeping Business Inner Circle" coaching program so that bookkeepers from all over the world can benefit from her experience and not struggle like she did.

She turned her personal experience into a profitable e-book for other bookkeepers. Once you have some experience, there's no reason why you can't share your own experiences, too!

Mike Sheldon is a freelance QuickBooks ProAdvisor in Northern California with a successful independent bookkeeping business. Mike was working as a bookkeeper for an employer when he decided to "break out" on his own. Mike is the owner-operator of Sheldon Enterprises.

He keeps up-to-date with developments in the accounting and bookkeeping field, and understands that good bookkeeping is essential to a client's success, even if his clients don't realize it themselves!

Mike spoke with us about his practice, his marketing strategies and tips, and how he manages his thriving bookkeepring business.

Case Study of Success: Interview with Sylvia Jaumann

Successful Freelance Bookkeeper, Writer, and Businesswoman

Sylvia Jaumann
Professional Bookkeeper and Author
"Secrets to Starting & Running Your Own Bookkeeping Business" e-book
www.1stratebooks.com
"Bookkeeping Business Inner Circle" Coaching Program
www.bookkeepingbusinesscoach.com
E-mail: admin@bookkeepingbusinesscoach.com

What was it that made you decide to start your own bookkeeping service?

Sylvia: I've pretty much always wanted my own business because I have a strong independent streak. I also got tired of working for bosses who didn't value my skills or pay me what I thought I was worth. Once I found out that I could be making $10 - $15 more per hour working for myself it seriously motivated me to launch my own bookkeeping business.

What were the very first steps you took in getting your business going; how did you get your very first client?

Sylvia: I struggled for the longest time with all the logistics I would need to run a freelance bookkeeping business. Getting a business license and setting up my office was a no-brainer for me. But when it came down to how I would keep track of all my clients, track my billing, and stay organized, I was immobilized with doubt and fear. I ended up subcontracting for another bookkeeper for a year and this helped me fill in all the blanks as I learned a ton of organizational skills from her.

I picked up my very first client through word of mouth. I've acquired the majority of my clients this way. I've done newspaper advertising and have received inquiries from potential clients, but I seem to find better quality clients through referrals from others.

How much experience and/or technical training as a bookkeeper did you have before starting your business?

Sylvia: I'd had about five years experience working for others before I felt confident enough in my abilities to venture out on my own. My formal education consisted of basic bookkeeping courses and an income tax preparation course. I've found that's all I've ever needed and it's worked well for me.

What are the three biggest mistakes you see people make when they try to start their own bookkeeping business?

Sylvia: Mistake #1: Undercharging for their bookkeeping services, thereby undercutting other local bookkeepers. Not only is this unfair to other bookkeepers, but it's a disservice to themselves. Generally, it's a lack of confidence that prompts bookkeepers to not charge enough for their services.

Mistake #2: Being so hungry for work that they accept every bookkeeping job that comes along, even those jobs that they should probably be taking a pass on. Bookkeeping jobs that involve a year's worth of paperwork stuffed in a box are not for the faint of heart. It can be very frustrating as many times critical information is missing. Then there are the clients who don't pay their bills. Many times you can't avoid this and only find this out after you've begun work on the project.

Mistake #3: Not requesting a retainer for new clients. This is a huge mistake made by bookkeepers who think that if they request money up front, the client will run. Most clients will not bat an eye if you request a retainer as long at it's reasonable. Lawyers and accountants demand them, so why shouldn't we?

What's the best way to avoid those mistakes, or to fix them if someone has already made them?

Sylvia: 1) Find out what other bookkeepers are charging and raise your rates accordingly. You may have to gradually increase your rates with existing clients.

2) If you discover that you've received a box of unsorted paperwork, request that the client organize it for you (unless you want to do it yourself). If you explain to the client the amount of money that they will save by sorting it out themselves, oftentimes they will do it.

3) Always request a retainer up front for new clients. If a client is not paying your bill on time and you've already taken him on, inform him that no further work will be done until your bill has been paid. Then get a retainer for all future work. Once the retainer is used up, request another one.

If a close friend came to you and asked for your advice on getting started with a bookkeeping service, what would you tell her or him?

Sylvia: I'd tell them about the organizational systems I've learned in keeping my clients on track. Setting up a system so that you always know at a glance what remittances need to be paid as well as being able to find important information at a moment's notice are crucial skills for freelance bookkeepers. Also, I'd tell them to always get a retainer up front before beginning any new bookkeeping jobs!

If you had it to do all over again, what would you do differently?

Sylvia: I would have taken the leap a lot sooner than I did. I wouldn't have let fear and doubt hold me back from living my dream. I wasted too many years working for other people and missed out financially because of this.

If you had to do it all over again, what would you do the same way?

Sylvia: I'd talk to people and not be afraid to mention that I have a bookkeeping business. I've obtained so many clients by just doing that one thing alone! Also, I'm not afraid to ask for referrals either.

What do you think are the biggest challenges facing our type of business today?

Sylvia: The biggest challenge I've come across are the mom and pop businesses where the mom (with no bookkeeping experience) ends up doing the bookkeeping herself in order to save money. These small business owners think that as long as they can learn an accounting program that they can easily do the bookkeeping. We all know this isn't the case. Then, at year end, the messes that have been created by the lack of experience ends up costing them more money by their accountants than if they'd let a competent bookkeeper handle it in the first place. It's frustrating when people aren't willing to invest in the essential expertise needed to run their business.

What's the biggest challenge you've faced in your business so far? How did you overcome it?

Sylvia: My biggest challenge was finding the self-confidence to actually make the leap into starting my own business. I knew how to do bookkeeping but had no idea how to manage many clients. I was worried about finding the right systems to keep track of all the work and possibly missing important remittances and deadlines. To overcome this, I ended up subcontracting for a bookkeeper for a year and learned many tricks and tips from her. It was a good educational experience for me and gave me a huge shot of confidence.

How long did it take you to get enough clients so that you were working full-time (or as many hours as you want)?

Sylvia: This is tricky because I'd had clients off and on for years before I finally decided to finally venture out on my own full-time. I'd say from the time I finally decided that I wanted to do this full-time to when I actually did was about eight months. During this time I gradually reduced my hours at my job.

What specific tools, websites, software, or services do you personally recommend for people who are trying to build their freelance business?

Sylvia: My favorite accounting program by far is Simply Accounting. I've used many other accounting programs but this one has been consistently the most user-friendly software I've ever used. I've used it since the beginning when it was called Bedford Accounting and was only available in DOS (I might be aging myself here). I also use Excel for all my spreadsheets (and I have a lot!) Then, of course, I use Word for all my documents like memos and letters.

I don't have a website in particular that I recommend for freelance bookkeepers other than creating your own bookkeeping service website. It took me a long time to justify the need for my own bookkeeping website. When it actually came time to set it up though, it only took me a few hours to make one. (I do have some experience in setting up websites though.) By adding my website link to local directories, it allows me free advertising exposure of my business name to other local businesses.

Do you have any "secret" tips, tricks, or techniques that you can share with us that very few people know about that will give us an edge in our field?

Sylvia: I don't know if this is much of a "secret," but a trick I use consistently is to set up as many recurring transactions as possible in each client's accounting data. I do this for bank charges, monthly debit charges that appear monthly on bank statements, vendor invoices, and even for deposits. Once I've figured out where something should be posted to, I don't want to have to look up the account number every time I post. This saves a ton of time and keeps me posting consistently to the same accounts.

If there was something you could have that you don't have right now that would make your freelancing business exactly the way you want it, what would it be?

Sylvia: My dream is to one day have a really beautiful office. Don't get me wrong, I have a decent office and working space right now. But it seems to me that since I spend so much time in my office that it really should be exactly the way I want it. I'd love to have an office with a sofa, maybe a small meeting area, and really nice, new furniture. Also, my office is in my basement so I'd love to have an office that's brighter with more natural light.

Case Study of Success: Interview with Mike Sheldon

Freelance Bookkeeper and Certified QuickBooks ProAdvisor®

Mike Sheldon, ProAdvisor®
Sheldon Enterprises
5341 Walnut Ave
Sacramento, CA 95841

Do you have a specific title that you use as a ProAdvisor?

Mike: Actually the certification for ProAdvisor gives me the right to use the insignia and the right to call myself a ProAdvisor. All that is trademarked [by Intuit], but I don't use an acronym.

Why did you decide to become a QuickBooks ProAdvisor?

Mike: Well, I'm a Washington, D.C. transplant. About five-and-a-half years ago, I worked for several companies and I was always asked to do the QuickBooks. I just happened to do this, and I was quite familiar with QuickBooks by the time I came to California. When I initially came to California, the job didn't pan out, so I decided to take what I knew and become certified and start my own bookkeeping practice. It was well worth it. When you become a QuickBooks ProAdvisor, you get online support and tech support—if there's something I don't know, I can find out.

Do you utilize the online support through QuickBooks via e-mail?

Mike: Well, you can do that, but the more immediate way is to request service by telephone. Sometimes there's a ten minute wait for support on the phone, but you get access to a different tier of help; there are armies of people helping you.

What do you like most about working in the financial industry?

Mike: I'm fascinated by all the exposure I'm getting from different businesses. There are people in those businesses that aren't trained, and they are overwhelmed by QuickBooks at first. By the time people call me, they are really frustrated. It's a nice feeling when you finally get a sigh of relief from your client, and they know they are going to get everything straightened out.

Even though clients feel that bookkeeping is necessary, it's not something that people look at as making them any money. They feel that bookkeeping is a waste of time, even if they need it badly. It's like taking out the trash—people know that it has to be done, but nobody likes to do it.

Do you want to expand your service or financial offerings?

Mike: I do want to expand. It doesn't matter what you do, you have to be a salesman, and marketing is easier for some people than others. My next target market is tax preparers and CPAs because helping them get what they want will help them and their clients better. CPAs don't want to do bookkeeping—the whole "shoebox full of receipts"—I'm sure that CPAs get calls all the time to do this type of work, but they don't want to do bookkeeping. It's just a matter of finding some that want to work with you.

Having good people skills is a good thing. I've got white collar professionals, attorneys, and blue collar truck drivers as clients. They are worlds apart in their needs, but you learn as you go along. Bookkeeping is bookkeeping; you just modify things as you go along and give clients what they want. It's a blessing when a prospective client already has a CPA, because it's already established what that CPA needs—we don't have to guess. It's a big plus when I can talk to a CPA and just make sure they are getting what they need.

When you were first starting out, what marketing tools did you use to generate clients?

Mike: The single most valuable marketing tool—well, it's more like advertising—is Craigslist. I get calls constantly and not all of them pan out, but it's just the idea that you have a free advertisement that you can re-post every couple of days.

I did a stupid thing and advertised in the Yellow Pages, and that wasn't cheap! It only generated two calls in a year. Needless to say, I won't be doing that again.

Maybe print advertising such as the yellow pages are becoming obsolete.

Mike: The only silver lining is that you also get in Yellowpages.com, but when you become a certified ProAdvisor, Intuit has a handshake deal with Google and when someone does a Google search, they find you at Intuit, so it's really great to become a ProAdvisor.

Do you have a website?

Mike: I have a website through Intuit; when I e-mail a client, I provide a link that goes right to my website, and clients can see information about me there.

How long did it take you to become a ProAdvisor?

Mike: With all the reading and quizzes, there are three major exams—it took me probably about thirteen hours. It's online, so you do it whenever when you can do it. Most people can get through it, and it was well worth it. I had QuickBooks experience, but the training program allows you to understand the theory behind the bookkeeping and the abstract thinking that you need to do.

Do you have a "busy season" or do you feel busy all year round?

Mike: It seems that my busiest times are from February to August. You might think that the end of the year would be the busiest because of tax time, but that's not it at all. Typically, after the beginning of a new year, people become resolute that they are going to "take the trash out," and finally get their bookkeeping done. When you're a bookkeeper, you're trading dollars for hours.

Tax time comes and goes, and there isn't a big rush with people that are trying to get the prior year together. There's a few of those, and if you get those, they're nice because it's a lot of hours—when their prior year bookkeeping is a mess. You have to start at the beginning and go through the whole thing, and that's nice. Other clients just need to know a few things and that's the last you'll hear from them. I have an orthodontist client who has a big practice—three locations and so there's a lot to be done there. He found me on Craigslist.

Chapter 11: Sample Forms and Letters

The following forms may be used freely without prior consent of the authors. You may distribute these forms for your own use only. These forms are informational only and not a substitute for legal advice. If you have legal questions, please consult a qualified attorney.

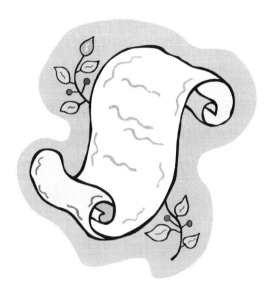

Sample (Easy) Business Plan for a Startup Bookkeeping and Tax Practice

A good business plan is absolutely essential to the success of your business. Even if you only brainstorm on these pages, every little bit of planning will help you succeed. The very act of planning your business's success helps you think critically about how to create real success for yourself and your future career as a tax or bookkeeping professional. Take the time to formulate your plan now and save yourself from costly mistakes later. It takes time now, but avoids costly, perhaps disastrous, mistakes later.

This business plan is a generic model for how to start, market, and maintain a successful bookkeeping and tax services business. It can be modified for tax practitioners or bookkeeping professionals. If you intend to add services to your practice, such as notary services, insurance sales, or other related products, you can add those to the existing lists. Cross out the services that you choose not to offer.

A good business plan takes anywhere from a few days to a few weeks to complete. That is because you will make many modifications to your business plan as you decide which services to offer and how you're going to market your services. Make notes as you decide on your changes. Those business owners who take the time to create a good business plan never regret the effort.

Great Bookkeeper, Inc.
(Sample Business Plan)

Owner: James Smith, CB

OWNERS
James Smith, CB
2122 Main St., Apt. #312
Cloverdale, TX 10000
Telephone 972-000-0000
Fax   1-800-000-0000

E-mail   GreatBookkeeper@yahoo.com

Executive Summary

Write this section last and make it brief.

Include everything that you would cover in a five-minute interview.
Explain the fundamentals of the proposed business. Make it concise.

Example:

Brief overview: Great Bookkeeper, Inc. is a bookkeeping and tax services company that offers various bookkeeping services to small businesses and individuals. Great Bookkeeper, Inc. specializes in bookkeeping for bakeries and restaurants. The owner, James Smith, was a long-time bookkeeper for Main Street Bakery and SunnySide Restaurant in Cloverdale, Texas. He has many years of experience in the industry.

Your brief overview:

_____
_____
_____

Mission statement: To offer exceptional bookkeeping and tax services to small businesses.

Your mission statement:

_____
_____
_____

Management: Owner: James Smith

Your management:

_____

Marketing: (Customer Base) Marketing will consist of direct marketing to all the local bakeries and restaurants. Great Bookkeeper, Inc. will also market its services on the Internet through our website, www.GreatBookkeeperInc.com. The business will also market to other potential businesses by using online classified ads to seek out employers who are looking for bookkeepers and bookkeeping services.

Your brief marketing statement:

_____
_____
_____
_____

Competition: There are currently three other bookkeeping services in the area. One business owner is not taking new clients, and one owner is looking to retire soon. So, essentially, we only have one competitor.

Your statement on the competition:

_____

_____

_____

Projections: Our projections are that this business has a great chance at success because there is little local competition, and the owner has many years of solid experience to make it a success.

Your brief statement on your market projections:

_____

_____

_____

General Company Description

Mission Statement: Great Bookkeeping, Inc. is dedicated to helping clients achieve financial success by devoting the time and attention that we believe you deserve.

Company goals and objectives:

Example: The goal of Great Bookkeeping, Inc. is to have a financially healthy, successful company that is a leader in customer service and that has a loyal customer following. Our sales objective is to obtain at least one new bookkeeping client every month, and grow the business until we reach a reasonable capacity of fifteen bookkeeping clients.

Target customers: To whom will you market your products?

_____

_____

Example: Marketing will consist of direct marketing to all the local bakeries and restaurants. Great Bookkeeper, Inc. will also market its services on the Internet through our website, www.GreatBookkeeperInc.com. The business will also market to other potential businesses by using online classified ads to seek out employers who are looking for bookkeepers and bookkeeping services.

Describe your most important company strengths and core competencies. What factors will make the company succeed? What do you think your major competitive strengths will be? What background experience, skills, and strengths do you personally bring to this new venture?
Legal form of ownership: Sole proprietorship, partnership, corporation, Limited Liability Corporation (LLC)?

Your company description:

_____

_____

_____

_____

_____

_____

_____

Products and Services

Describe in depth your products or services:

Example: Great Bookkeeping, Inc. is dedicated to helping clients achieve financial success by devoting the time and attention that we believe they deserve. We offer full-service bookkeeping and payroll, as well as monthly reports and bank reconciliations.

What are the fees of your bookkeeping or tax services??

Hourly or Flat rate?

_____

Example:

Services	Hourly Rate
Bookkeeping and financial reporting	$50
Financial consulting services	$50
Business management	$75
Accounts payable	$50
Accounts receivable and invoice billing	$50
General check writing functions	Varies
Payroll & compliance deposits and reporting	$50
Bank reconciliations-checkbook to bank	$50
General ledger maintenance	$50
Daily cash balance updating	$55
Monthly, quarterly, or yearly write-up	$75
Financial statements	$50
Yearly tax preparation	$100

Marketing Plan

Market research:

No matter how good your product and your service, the venture cannot succeed without effective marketing. And this begins with careful, systematic research. It is very dangerous to assume that you already know about your intended market. You need to do market research to make sure you're on track. Use the business planning process as your opportunity to uncover data and to question your marketing efforts. Your time will be well spent.

Customers:

Identify your targeted customers, their characteristics, and their geographic locations, otherwise known as their demographics. You may have more than one customer group.

Example: Our target customers will be small businesses, especially bakeries and restaurants that require bookkeeping and payroll services. The business will also market to other potential businesses, by using online classified ads to seek out employers who are looking for bookkeepers and bookkeeping services.

List your major competitors and describe how your products or services compare with the competition.

My competition:

_____
_____
_____

Now write a short paragraph stating your competitive advantages and disadvantages:

_____
_____
_____

Niche:

Do you plan to market your bookkeeping and tax services to a particular group of customers, such as clergy, nonprofits, etc.? In one short paragraph, define your niche—your unique corner of the market.

_____
_____

Promotion and Advertising

How will you get the word out to customers?
Advertising: Have you identified low-cost methods to get the most out of your promotional budget?

Will you use methods other than paid advertising, such as trade shows, catalogs, dealer incentives, word of mouth (how will you stimulate it?), and network of friends or professionals?

What image do you want to project? How do you want customers to see you?

Your plan to promote and advertise your bookkeeping business:

_____
_____
_____
_____
_____

Promotional Budget:
How much will you spend on the items listed above?

_____
_____
_____
_____
_____

Operational Plan

Managing Your Accounts Receivable

If you plan to extend credit, you should do an aging at least monthly to track how much of your money is tied up in credit given to customers and to alert you to slow payment problems. You must decide the following:

After an invoice becomes late:
- When do you make a phone call?
- When do you send a letter?
- When do you discontinue services and send the client to collections?

Managing Your Accounts Payable

You should also age your accounts payable—what you owe to your suppliers. This helps you plan whom to pay and when. Paying too early depletes your cash, but paying late can cost you valuable discounts and can damage your credit. (Hint: If you know you'll be late making a payment, call the creditor before the due date.)

Startup Expenses and Capitalization

It's important to estimate these expenses accurately and then to plan where you will get sufficient capital. This is a research project, and the more thorough your research efforts, the less chance that you will leave out important expenses or underestimate them.

Even with the best of research, however, opening a new business has a way of costing more than you anticipate. There are two ways to make allowances for surprise expenses. The first is to add a little "padding" to each item in the budget. The problem with that approach, however, is that it destroys the accuracy of your carefully wrought plan. The second approach is to add a separate line item, called contingencies, to account for the unforeseeable. This is the approach we recommend.

Talk to others who have started similar businesses to get a good idea of how much to allow for contingencies. If you cannot get good information, we recommend a rule of thumb that contingencies should equal at least 20 percent of the total of all other startup expenses.

Explain your research and how you arrived at your forecasts of expenses. Give sources, amounts, and terms of proposed loans. Also explain in detail how much will be contributed by each

Sample Introductory Letter to New Client

Ms. Ima Accurate
The Accurate Bookkeeper, Inc.
Jiminy Christmas, CA, 92110

June 30, 2010
Mr. Daniel G. Smith
Timberlake Construction, Inc.
1000 Main Street
Taneytown, CA 95810

Dear Mr. Smith:
I saw your recently posted employment ad on Craigslist {insert the source of your referral here}. I would like to offer your company my services as a full-charge bookkeeper. I am confident that you will be very satisfied with my services.

With my services, your business will enjoy the advantage of accurate bookkeeping and financial reports without the costs involved with employing a full or part-time accountant. I understand the hard work it takes to make a small business succeed. I enjoy the unique challenges that a small business offers. I can produce monthly financials, provide insight on how to help your business, forecast cash flow, and provide a wide range of bookkeeping and tax services.

Outsourcing your bookkeeping and accounting will save you money in a variety of ways. Your business can save an overall of 70 percent on salary and overhead compared with hiring an employee bookkeeper. Removing the mundane bookkeeping tasks off your plate also gives you more time to generate revenue from your own customers.

The information enclosed will help you make the most of my services. If you have questions, please contact me. As your needs change, I will be happy to help you evaluate those needs and offer you the services that will help you achieve your new goals. Thank you for your consideration.

Sincerely,

Ima Accurate, CB
Company President
The Accurate Bookkeeper, Inc.
Direct: 916-000-0000

Enclosure: List of Financial Services

Sample Introductory Letter to a Potential Client (Referral)

Ms. Ima Accurate
The Accurate Bookkeeper, Inc.
Jiminy Christmas, CA, 92110

June 30, 2010
Mrs. Janice Green
Janice's Fabric Stores, Inc.
300 B Street
Quilting Town, CA 81000

Dear Mrs. Green:
You and your company have been recommended to me by Mr. Stephen Jones of Hardcore Cycling Co., who indicated that you may be interested in the bookkeeping and tax services provided by my company. I am confident that you will be very satisfied with my services.

I have enclosed my list of bookkeeping and tax services. I will be in the Quilting Town area the week of July 16. I would like to meet with you to discuss how my bookkeeping and tax services can help your business be more profitable and save more money on taxes. I will contact you within the next ten days to schedule an appointment. In the meantime, if you have any questions, call me at (916) 000-0000. I look forward to meeting you.

Sincerely,
Ima Accurate, CB
Company President
The Accurate Bookkeeper, Inc.
Direct: 916-000-0000

Enclosure: List of Financial Services

Sample List of Services (Chart)

Comprehensive bookkeeping services:	Financial statement preparation:
Complete payroll management, including all associated federal and state electronic tax filings Complete accounts receivable and billing Accounts payable Sales tax reporting Bank statement reconciliation QuickBooks setup	Profitability projections Balance sheet Income statement Cash flow statement Budgets
Tax Services:	
Quarterly estimated federal and state tax filing 1099 tax reporting W-2 preparation Compilation at year end of all documentation required for CPA tax preparation Preparation of annual corporate filings with city agencies	

Sample List of Services (Simple)

Our Complete Bookkeeping and Tax Services

The Accurate Bookkeeper, Inc. offers complete financial solutions for small businesses just like yours!

We offer complete:

- Bookkeeping and financial reporting
- Financial consulting services
- Business management
- Accounts payable
- Accounts receivable and invoice billing
- General check writing functions
- Payroll & compliance deposits and reporting
- Bank reconciliations-checkbook to bank
- General ledger maintenance
- Daily cash balance updating
- Monthly, quarterly, or yearly write-up
- Financial statements
- Yearly tax preparation

Through a careful analysis process, I seek to understand your business challenges and provide customized bookkeeping and tax services that will maximize your profits and help you reach your financial goals.

For more information, please call:

Ima Accurate, CB
Company President
The Accurate Bookkeeper, Inc.
Direct: 916-000-0000
Fax: 1-800-000-0000
www.ImaAccurate.com

Sample Engagement Letter (Bookkeeping)

Engagement Letter
Ima Accurate, CB
Company President
The Accurate Bookkeeper, Inc.
Direct: 916-000-0000
Fax: 1-800-000-0000

Dear _(client)___,

Thank you for selecting our company to assist you with your financial affairs. This letter confirms the terms of our engagement with you and the nature and extent of services we will provide. As we discussed, beginning on ___(date)_____ I will do the following work for you each month:

1. Reconcile your checkbook and bank statements, identify errors and specific sources of adjustments, inform you of these adjustments, and request that you make correcting entries directly into your checkbook.
2. Review and prepare your payroll records and payroll tax deposits. For any error I find I will take appropriate action as required to correct such errors.
3. Record all income and expenses, deposits, and adjusting entries needed for that month.
4. Quarterly, I will prepare your state and federal unemployment tax returns. You agree to provide the required forms to send to state and federal offices.

It is your responsibility to provide information required for preparation of complete and accurate books. You should keep all documents, canceled checks, and other data that support your reported income and deductions. They may be necessary to prove accuracy and completeness of the returns to a taxing authority. The monthly bookkeeping fees will be $_____.

If you would like me to perform additional services, I will be pleased to do so, but they are not included in this letter or the accompanying estimate.

By signing below I have agreed to accept the services above at the stated fees.

_____

Client Signature and Date

_____

Ima Accurate, CB
The Accurate Bookkeeper, Inc.

Sample Engagement Letter, Simple (Tax Preparation)

Your fee at the time of the preparation of your tax return will include the following services at no extra charge:

- Preparation of both federal and state tax returns, complete with envelopes for mailing (if not e-filed)
- A customer copy of the tax return for your records
- If you receive any correspondence from the IRS or the State Tax Board, we will respond to the inquiries for any tax returns we have completed.

Additional fees may be charged for the following services:
If we provide further tax planning consultations beyond the initial tax appointment, or provide a W-4 write-up during the year, we will charge an additional fee based on our hourly rate.
If you need additional assistance during an audit, either in IRS offices or our office, we will charge an additional fee based on the services rendered.

We assume that you have given us all the correct and necessary information to process the tax return. If there is any missing information, we will notify you in writing. We urge you to read through your return and if you have any questions concerning its contents, please request a follow-up interview to review it.

If you receive any inquiries or letters from the IRS or State Tax Board, please contact us as soon as you receive the notice. We will assist you with this correspondence and will communicate with the agencies when necessary.

Signed_____ Date _____

Signed_____ Date _____

Sample Engagement Letter, Extended (Tax Preparation)

Engagement Letter for Preparation of Individual Tax Returns

Dear ___(Client)_____:

Thank you for selecting ___(your company)___ to assist you with your tax returns. In order to minimize any possible misunderstandings as to the scope of the work that you want me to do for you and the payment for such services, this Engagement Letter sets forth our understanding regarding the assignment and constitutes our agreement as to the scope of the services and the fees for such services. Please be sure that this letter does in fact reflect your expectations before returning a signed copy to me.

We will prepare your ___(tax year)_____ federal and all state income tax returns you request using information you provide to us. We may ask for clarification of some items, but we will not audit or otherwise verify the data you submit.

Tax return preparation may require other tax and accounting services. We will depend on the information you are supplying as being accurate and complete to the best of your knowledge, and we will rely on your representation that you have maintained the documentation required by law to support your expenses for meals, entertainment, travel, gifts, vehicle use, and charitable contributions. We will not verify the information you provide, but we may ask you for clarification of some data.

It is your responsibility to provide information required for preparation of complete and accurate returns. You should keep all documents, canceled checks, and other data that support your reported income and deductions. They may be necessary to prove accuracy and completeness of the returns to a taxing authority. You are responsible for the returns, so you should review them carefully before you sign them.

Our work will not include any procedures to discover omissions or other irregularities. The only accounting or analysis work we will do is that which is necessary for preparation of your income tax returns.

We must use our judgment in resolving questions where the tax law is unclear, or where there may be conflicts between the taxing authorities' interpretations of the law and other supportable positions. In order to avoid penalties, we will apply the "more likely than not" reliance standard to resolve such issues. You agree to honor our decisions regarding the need to make protective disclosures in your returns.

The law also imposes penalties when taxpayers understate their tax liability. If you have concerns about such penalties, please call us. Your returns may be selected for audit by a taxing authority. Any proposed adjustments are subject to appeal.

Our fee for preparation of your tax returns will be based on the amount of time required at standard billing rates plus out-of-pocket expenses. All invoices are due and payable upon presentation. To the extent permitted by state law, an interest charge may be added to all accounts not paid within thirty (30) days.

The IRS may disagree with my conclusions or opinions so we will only be responsible for refunds of fees where we have failed to inform you of the potential consequences of pursuing a particular course of action or series of transactions.

We will retain copies of records you supplied to us along with our work papers for your engagement for a period of seven years. After seven years, our work papers and engagement files will be destroyed. All of your original records will be returned to you at the end of this engagement. You should keep the original records in secure storage.

To affirm that this letter correctly summarizes your understanding of the arrangements for this work, please sign the enclosed copy of this letter in the space indicated. We appreciate your confidence in us. Please call if you have questions.

Sincerely,

_____
Sandy Superior, EA, CB
Company President
The Superior Financial, Inc.

Accepted By: (Client) _____   Date _____

(Client) _____   Date _____

Sample Subcontractor Agreement

Subcontractor name: Jenny Jones
Street address: 123 Main St, Anytown, CA, 12345
Phone number: 916-123-4567
Today's date: _____

Scope of work to be performed by subcontractor: Bookkeeping and Tax Preparation services.
Specifications of project: Will be provided at the beginning of each project.

Required completion date and time: Will be provided with each project. Late completions will result in a five dollar per hour reduction in payment to subcontractor for every 12 hours past due. Subcontractor must notify _____ (client) immediately upon subcontractor's realization that the project will be late.

Hourly rate of payment to subcontractor: "RATE"

Maximum hours to be paid: Will be provided with each project.

Subcontractor acknowledges and agrees that all information derived from the work to be performed is strictly confidential and shall not be conveyed to any third party at any time.

Subcontractor further acknowledges that the proprietor or owner of the source material of which this agreement is the subject is the client of _____ obtained through its own marketing and work efforts. Subcontractor agrees not to contact such proprietor or owner for the purposes of solicitation of subcontractor's services for a period of one year from the required completion date herein.

Accepted By: (Client) _____   Date _____

(Client) _____   Date _____

Resources

Professional Organizations

American Institute of Professional Bookkeepers

www.aipb.org

The most widely respected national bookkeeping association and certification, established in 1987. The board members are highly respected members of the financial community—this organization was founded by two Certified Public Accountants, Stanley Hartman and Stephen Sahlein.

National Association of Enrolled Agents (NAEA)

www.naea.org

The NAEA is a national association of over 11,000 independent, licensed tax professionals called Enrolled Agents (EA). They are the largest national organization dedicated just to Enrolled Agents. They offer a wide range of membership benefits including CPE and the well-known publication, *The EA Journal*. Every member automatically joins the national chapter when he or she joins a state chapter.

National Association of Tax Professionals (NATP)

www.natptax.com

The largest association of tax professionals, founded in 1979. Members include unenrolled practitioners, Enrolled Agents, accountants, CPAs, attorneys, and financial planners. NATP offers a tax resource and education center. They offer year-round CPE. NATP has a tax store that sells tax prep materials (such as folders and client newsletters).

They also offer the NATP Tax Professional Fee Study, which is a yearly fee study that's worth the price of membership alone. Find out what other preparers around the country are charging and what software they use: very good information.

National Society of Accountants (NSA)

(Formerly the NSPA)

www.nsacct.org

Originally started in 1945, NSA has a membership of 12,000. Today, the NSA continues to support the Enrolled Agent program by offering an Enrolled Agent preparatory course. In 1973, the NSA established ACAT (Accreditation Council for Accountancy and Taxation) as an independent credentialing body to provide a standard of competency in the area of public accounting.

In 1976, NSA launched the National Accounting Forum, a two-day program featuring sixteen hours of CPE. Later, to help its members provide high quality professional services, the NSA introduced the National Estate Tax conferences and the ACAT Review Course.

National Society of Tax Professionals

www.nstp.org

The NSTP was founded in 1985. Membership is open to most practicing financial professionals. The NSTP offers a wide range of membership benefits, including CPE and discounts on products.

Education and Licensing Resources

Accreditation Council for Accountancy and Taxation® (ACAT)

www.acatcredentials.org

ACAT credentials are a valuable way to raise proficiencies, earn professional recognition, gain a competitive edge, boost business and jumpstart careers. There are four designations offered:

- Accredited Business Accountant® (ABA)
- Accredited Tax Advisor® (ATA)
- Accredited Tax Preparer® (ATP)
- Elder Care Specialist™ (ECS)

A proficiency exam, experience requirement, and continuing education are required for each designation. You must also agree to adhere to a code of ethics.

QuickBooks ProAdvisor® Program

www.proadvisor.intuit.com

The QuickBooks ProAdvisor program is well respected by the general public and accounting professionals alike. Many Enrolled Agents become ProAdvisors and continue to renew their certification every year. Many EAs report that Intuit's ProAdvisor program is a constant source of referrals year after year.

Thompson Prometric

www.prometric.com

Thompson Prometric is the exclusive administrator of the IRS Enrolled Agent exam. Prometric has testing centers all over the United States. Accommodations are available for disabled students. You can find out more about the IRS EA exam by going to Prometric's website. You may schedule your appointment for the testing period May 1- February 28. There is no testing in March and April.

Universal Accounting Center

www.universalaccounting.com

The Universal Accounting Center trains accountants, tax preparers, and bookkeepers. They offer practice building, tax preparer training, and QuickBooks' courses. They offer professional designations, such as the Professional Bookkeeper (PB) and Professional Tax Preparer (PTP).

Even if you are already a tax professional, these additional designations can help raise your profile and increase your marketability.

Index

Subcontractors, 80

T

Tax deduction
    Ethics of, 70
    Home office, 37
    Mileage, 24
    Records requirement, 79
Tax preparation, 31
Tax services, 67
Tax software, 69
Tax training, 68
Telemarketing, 50
Telephone, 26
Thompson Prometric, 128
Time management, 18
Training, 68

Trust fund recovery, 77

U

Universal Accounting Center, 129

V

Vistaprint, 25

W

Website, 56
Weekend syndrome, 19
WordPress, 56

About the Authors

About Gabrielle Fontaine, PB

Gabrielle Fontaine, PB is a freelance Professional Bookkeeper as well as a QuickBooks trainer and consultant who provides her services exclusively on a virtual basis, using only the Internet and telephone to work with her clients. Gabrielle's official website is: *www.BookkeepingDirect.com.*

Gabrielle attained her designation as a Professional Bookkeeper from Universal Accounting Institute, and has Advanced Certification on QuickBooks as a ProAdvisor through Intuit, Inc., the makers of QuickBooks financial software. She is a member of the American Institute of Professional Bookkeepers (AIPB), the National Association of Certified Professional Bookkeepers (NACPB), and the National Association of Tax Professionals (NATP).

She has over eighteen years of freelance business experience and is a nationally published writer of business articles, reports, and an industry-specific business operations manual. She is also the publisher of the highly praised, FREE online newsletter, The Freelance Bookkeeper, designed especially for new and aspiring bookkeepers who are ready to turn their recordkeeping skills into a profitable freelance business. To learn more, visit *www.TheFreelanceBookkeeper.com.*

About Christy Pinheiro, EA ABA®

Christy Pinheiro is an Enrolled Agent, Accredited Business Advisor®, and financial writer. She is the author of multiple books on taxation, bookkeeping, and management. Her finance and tax articles have been nationally published online and in various periodicals. She is a member of the National Association of Tax Professionals and the National Association of Enrolled Agents. She has a tax practice in Sacramento.

Her website is *www.ChristyPinheiro.com.*

Are You Interested in Becoming an Enrolled Agent?

Passkey EA Review
www.PassKeyPublications.com

PassKey EA Review has a full range of study materials for the IRS Enrolled Agent exam. Available for the 2010 exam year, PassKey EA Review has self-paced study materials that will give you the knowledge and training to pass the exam the first time. We extract key points of the exam, and provide you with exercises, questions, and tips on passing the exam.

Let us help you become an Enrolled Agent, the most widely respected tax designation in the world! See the full selection of books and study materials at *www.PassKeyPublications.com*.

A new edition is released every year, right in time for the IRS's release date for the new EA exam.

The Freelance Bookkeeper

Attention: Professional bookkeepers (or those who want to be)...

"Finally! The Single Greatest Source of Tips, Tricks, Tools and Just Plain Truth About Breaking Free and Becoming A Highly Paid Freelance Bookkeeper"

"The Freelance Bookkeeper" is a new FREE online multimedia newsletter loaded with no-fluff, cut-to-the-chase, real life information that you can use immediately to build your own highly profitable freelance bookkeeping practice:

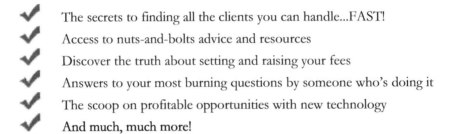

- The secrets to finding all the clients you can handle...FAST!
- Access to nuts-and-bolts advice and resources
- Discover the truth about setting and raising your fees
- Answers to your most burning questions by someone who's doing it
- The scoop on profitable opportunities with new technology
- And much, much more!

If you are serious about truly making it as a freelance bookkeeper, then you NEED to subscribe to this newsletter NOW!

Visit: **www.TheFreelanceBookkeeper.com** to get your FREE subscription.

Endnotes

[1] Various classifieds, Sacramento Bee, Craigslist, Careerbuilder

[2] Price comparison, QuickBooks website and other retailers. 2009-2010 pricing.

[3] The authors do not receive any compensation or consideration for the websites or products mentioned in this book.

[4] The authors do not receive any compensation or consideration for the websites or products mentioned in this book.

[5] NATP tax preparer survey, 2009.

[6] IRS Office of Program Evaluation and Risk Analysis, Paid Preparer Review for National Public Liaison (Sept. 2007).

[7] Names have been changed.

Made in the USA
Lexington, KY
28 February 2012